A LA MODE

A LA MODE

On the Social Psychology of Fashion

René König

Translated by F. Bradley

With an Introduction by Tom Wolfe

A CONTINUUM BOOK
The Seabury Press • New York

THE SEABURY PRESS
815 Second Avenue
New York, N.Y. 10017

This translation © George Allen & Unwin Ltd 1973
Introduction Copyright © 1973 by Tom Wolfe
Printed in the United States of America

Original edition: *Macht und Reiz der Mode,* © 1971
Econ Verlag GmbH, Düsseldorf and Vienna

All rights reserved. No part of this book may be reproduced in any form, except for brief reviews, without the written permission of the publisher.

ISBN: 0-8164-9163-1

For Irmgard

A LA MODE

Preface

Fashion has a strange fascination: once it has aroused your interest you are forever under its spell. At least this is my own experience.

It caught me quite unawares; in Zurich many years ago I gave a lecture on fashion which, unlike many other events, I still vividly remember. In fact I returned to the subject again and again and developed from it a number of publications, among them *Collected Papers* in Zurich in 1958, and a short book in Germany in 1968. This book represents a further development, of which its much wider scope is evidence.

There is much discussion today of the collaboration of several branches of science in the analysis of certain subjects. What we have mainly in mind are weighty problems such as the development of modern society in general, of the Third World, or of the economy; but we are apt to forget the most outstanding example of such interdisciplinary collaboration: the question of fashion. This constitutes a point at which the methods of economics, psychology, sociology, social psychology, depth psychology and psychoanalysis, anthropology and ethology (animal and human) converge. Fashion is a wide-ranging social phenomenon requiring a wide range of perspectives for its understanding. I have tried to keep this principle in sight throughout the book.

Another difficulty arises in the discussion of the problem of fashion. I quote later on a roguish exchange from one of Shakespeare's plays which says that fashion makes 'giddy' anyone who is concerned with it. Of this, indeed, one must beware. To find out the tricks of fashion one must not lose oneself too much in it. Whoever clings to a certain form of fashion is by necessity always out of date. It can not, therefore, be the purpose of this book to praise individual fashions, but to reveal what they have in common throughout history.

How significant these common features are is for the reader to decide. What I myself aimed to do was to approach the phenomenon without any bias and to illuminate it from as many directions as possible.

R.K.

Contents

Preface		*page* 9
Introduction by Tom Wolfe		15
1	For and Against Fashion	29
2	Fashion-oriented Behaviour – Content and Form	37
3	The All-embracing Reality of Fashion	40
4	Change and Stability	53
5	Roots and Branches	66
6	Fashion-oriented Behaviour in Animals and Children	69
7	Novelty, Curiosity and the New Look	76
8	To See and to be Seen	81
9	Decoration and Distinction	84
10	Recognition	95
11	Rivalry and Competition	101
12	Conspicuousness and Approval	111
13	Imitation	116
14	Performers and Spectators	122
15	Ceremonial Behaviour and Etiquette	128
16	The Process of Civilization and Modesty	133
17	The First Spread of Fashion-oriented Behaviour	139
18	Fashion in the Bourgeois Moneyed Circles	146
19	Male Puritanism Versus Female Fashion	154
20	Fashion Captures the Masses	165
21	The Spread of Fashion in Today's Society	176
22	Old Techniques Produce New Fashions	185
23	First Interlude: Topless or Not?	193
24	Second Interlude: Fashion and Anti-fashion	198

25	Fashion and Mass Consumption	209
26	The Expansion of the Consumer Field	216
27	The New Line	221

Select Bibliography 227
Index 233

Illustrations

		facing page
1	Tanagra figure of a noble Greek lady in chiton and cloak	32
2	Madame Grès, the great Paris *couturière*, at work	32
3	Egyptian dancers, about 1500 B.C.	33
4	Antique bikini, imperial villa in Sicily	33
5	Noblewoman, Middle Ages	48
6	Jost Amman: Woman, Strasbourg 1577	48
7	An old document dealing with the topless question	49
8	Topless fashion, young woman, about 1750	49
9	Frans Hals, Regents of St Elizabeth, 1641; classical example of middle-class men's fashion	80
10	Women's fashion (about 1895)	81
11	Women's fashion (1896)	81
12	Madame Récamier (by David), the Queen of the Directoire	96
13	High Society: Mr and Mrs Hobson at the races, Paris 1914	97
14	A hippie couple, Isle of Man Pop Festival (1970)	97
15	Juliette Greco in a black jumper	144
16	An admirer takes leave kissing the lady's hand (1777)	145
17	Full-length evening gown by Balenciaga, Spring 1957	160
18	See-through fashions by Mary Quant (1969)	161
19	Trouser suit by Courréges (1964)	176
20	A simple version of the bikini (1971)	177
21	Simple minidress (1971)	192
22	Hot pants, London (1971)	193

Introduction
by Tom Wolfe

I first noticed the fashion I think of as Funky Chic one night in October of 1969 in London in a club called Arethusa, which was a favorite spot of the *bon ton*. A man comes rushing into the Gents and squares off in front of a mirror, removes his tie and stuffs it into a pocket of his leather coat, jerks open the top four buttons of his shirt, shoves his fingers in under the hair on top of his head and starts thrashing and tousling it into a ferocious disarray, steps back and appraises the results, turns his head this way and that, pulls his shirt open a little wider to let the hair on his chest sprout out, and then, seeing that everything is just so, heads in toward the dining-room for the main event. This dining-room is a terrific place. It has just been done over in the white plaster arches and conical lamps of the smart restaurant decor of that time known as Expense Chit Trattoria. In the grand salon only the waiters wear white shirts and black ties. The clientele sit there roaring and gurgling and flashing fireproof grins in a rout of leather jerkins, Hindu tunics, buckskin skirts, deerslayer boots, dueling shirts, bandannas knotted at the Adam's apple, love beads dangling to the belly, turtlenecks reaching up to meet the muttonchops at midjowl, Indian blouses worn thin and raggy to reveal the jutting nipples and crimson aureolae underneath ... The place looks like some grand luxe dining-room on the Mediterranean unaccountably overrun by mob-scene scruffs from out of *Northwest Passage*, *The Informer*, *Gunga Din* and *Bitter Rice*. What I was gazing upon was in fact the full fashion splendor of London's *jeunesse dorée*, which by 1969, of course, included everyone under the age of 67 with a taste for the high life.

Funky Chic came skipping and screaming into the United States the following year in the form of such marvelous figures as the Debutante in Blue Jeans. She was to be found on the fashion pages in every city of any size in the country. There she is in the photograph . . . wearing her blue jeans and her blue work shirt, open to the sternum, with her long pre-Raphaelite hair parted on top of the skull, uncoifed but recently washed and blown dry with a Continental Pro Style dryer (the Word-of-mouth that year said the Continental gave more 'body') . . . and she is telling her interviewer: 'We're not having any "coming out balls" this year or any "deb parties" or any of that. We're fed up with doing all the same old things, which are so useless, and seeing the same old faces and dancing to so-called "society bands" while a lot of old ladies in orange-juice-colored dresses stand around the edges talking to our parents. We're tired of cotillions and hunt cups and weekends. You want to know what I did last weekend? I spent last weekend at the day care center, looking after the most beautiful black children . . . and *learning* from them!'

Or as a well-known full-grown socialite, Amanda Burden, said at that time: 'The sophistication of the baby blacks has made me rethink my attitudes.' Whereupon she described herself as 'anti-fashion'.

Anti-fashion! Terrific. Right away anti-fashion itself became the most raving fashion imaginable . . . also known as Funky Chic. Everybody had sworn off fashion, but somehow nobody moved to Cincinnati to work among the poor. Instead, everyone stayed put and imported the poor to the fashion pages. That's the way it happened! For it was in that same year, 1970, that Funky Chic evolved into its most exquisite manifestation, namely, Radical Chic, which I have had occasion to describe elsewhere . . . Socialites began to give parties for the Black Panthers, for example, at their homes, from Park Avenue to Croton-on-Hudson. Which is to say, they began to bring exotic revolutionaries into their living-rooms and thereby achieved the ultimate in Funky Chic interior decoration: live black bodies.

It was at this point that fashion, on the one hand, and politics, ideology and philosophy, on the other, began to interlock in a most puzzling way. The fashion of Radical Chic swept not only socialites but also intellectuals and cultivated persons of every sort in the years 1968–70. The situation began to contradict the conventional assumption of historians, which is that fashion is but the embroidery of history, if that. It is true that Radical Chic would have never become a fashion if certain political ideas and emotions had not already been in the air. But once Radical Chic became fashionable, it took on its own momentum. It had the power to create political change on its own – i.e. many influential people who had been generally apolitical began to express support for groups like the Panthers. Was the process that brought them to that point really any different from the process that a few years before might have induced them to choose a new shirt length or a narrower waist silhouette?

This is the sort of question that fascinates Professor René König. His thesis is that fashion is as profound and critical a part of the social life of man as sex . . . and is made up of the same ambivalent mixture of irresistible urges and inevitable taboos . . . He insists that 'fashion is not merely a superficial – decorative or disfiguring – feature of life' but is 'an important regulator and means of expression within the community of men'. And he goes further. He says that not only man's status in his community but also the way he expresses himself – and even his very self-image – has depended 'from the very beginning of his existence as a species to a truly astonishing extent on that mysterious force we simply call fashion'.

This is not a thesis that is likely to get a very charitable reception just now, among scholars or readers generally. If the Boubon Louises may be said to have lived in the Age of Absolutism, we now live in the Age of Egalitarianism (with the emphasis on the *ism* rather than the facts, if one need edit). Even people who lend themselves to the fashion pages, the people whose faces run through *Vogue, Bazaar, Harper's Bazaar & Queen* and *Town & Country* like a bolt of crisp white glazed chintz, are not going to be caught out today talking about fashion in terms of *being fashionable*. They talk instead of ease, comfort, convenience, practicality, simplicity, and, occasionally, fun and gaiety (for others to share). Right now I am looking at a page of photographs in *Bazaar* of a woman named Venetia Barker, a young English matron whose husband owns a stable of horses and a fleet of helicopters. She tells how two or three times a week she flies her own canary-yellow helicopter from their country home in Wiltshire to their townhouse in London in order to go antique-hunting. Twice a week she flies it to Worcestershire to go horseback riding in the fox hunts. She speaks of the helicopter as a time-saving convenience, however, and of fox hunting in terms of mental hygiene: two days a week with horse & hound beats the psychiatrist any time in coping with the pressures of a busy modern life. 'During the day,' she says, 'I wear what's most practical', items such as a Regency coachman's cape with three huge layers of flapping red overlaps about the shoulders plus leather pants by Foale and Tuffin of London. At night she changes 'into something quite simple', which turns out to be outfits such as a black tunic gown by the good Madame Grés, slashed on the sides to reveal a floor-length scarlet slip and cross-laced black drawstrings, and surmounted at the bosom by a filigree diamond necklace with an emerald pendant the size of a brazil nut. Convenience, health, practicality, simplicity ... none of which means that the woman is being hypocritical or even cagey. She is merely observing a convention, a fashion taboo that is common to people at every level of income and status today.

The curious thing is that the same taboo makes fashion an even touchier subject for scholars. Louis Auchincloss once observed that academic writers seem to find the courage to write about society, in the sense of fashionable society, only from a great distance – either from across an ocean or across a gulf of a century or more in time, and preferably both. 'Why can we find a hundred professors eager to explore the subtleties of the court of the Empress Theodora,' he asks, 'and not one to plumb the depths of a party given by Perle Mesta?' He also remarked, quite aptly, I would say, that nothing offers a more revealing insight into the character of the high tide of American capitalism than the social life of Newport in the 1890s – 'a crazy patchwork of borrowed values financed on a scale that would have made the Sun King stare' – and to this day the one serious study of it is by a Frenchman, Paul Bourget.

Auchincloss is a novelist, of course, and ever since the time of Richardson and Fielding, some 230 years ago, novelists have been drawn to fashion as an essential ingredient of realistic narration. This was out of sheer instinct and not theory. Early in the game they seemed to sense that fashion is a code, a symbolic vocabulary that offers a sub-rational but instant and very brilliant illumination of the characters of individuals and even entire periods, especially periods of great turmoil. Professor König expresses this on a theoretical level by saying: 'In fashion the dynamic component is predominant, so that its cultural significance will be particularly prominent when sudden spasms of movement begin to transform a traditional system.' And yet novelists who have dwelled on fashion in just this way have usually been regarded in their own time as lightweights – 'trivial' has been the going word – scarcely even literary artists, in fact; even those who eventually have been judged to be the literary giants of their eras. Doctor Johnson dismissed Fielding as minor, trivial, unserious, to the very end. He could not understand how any serious writer could wallow so contentedly in the manners and mores, the everyday habits, of so many rascals, high and low. Saint-Beuve continually compared Balzac to people like antique dealers, sellers of women's clothes and – this was one of his favorites – the sort of down-at-the-heel petty bourgeois doctors who make house calls and become community gossips. Saint-Beuve detested the way the minutiae of fashion became crucial ingredients in Balzac's very mode of creating character. Balzac was not regarded as a major writer until after his death; he was not even invited to join the French Academy.

In our own time I don't have the slightest doubt but what Evelyn Waugh will eventually stand as England's only major novelist of the twentieth century (oh, all right, him and Lawrence). But during the last decade of his life his stock sank very low, so low, in fact, that he seemed finally to downgrade himself, judging by the opening chapter of *The Ordeal of Gilbert Pinfold*. In his writing he immersed himself so deeply in the fashions of his times that many critics regarded him as a snob first and an artist second. (I recall one reviewer who became furious because Waugh had the hero of his final trilogy, Guy Crouchback, describe his father's funeral mainly in terms of how correctly everyone was dressed despite the fact that it was wartime and the funeral was in the country.) John O'Hara's reputation has undergone a similar deflation over the past fifteen years. As for Louis Auchincloss – he has more than once set in motion characters who pursue the lure of Wall Street & Wealth & Family & Men's Club in the most relentless manner – only to see critics complain that the character is not believable: people don't conduct their lives that way any more. Auchincloss complains with some annoyance that they are saying 'don't' when what they mean is 'shouldn't'.

Auchincloss identifies the moral objection that underlies the taboo as follows. At the very core of fashionable society exists a monstrous vulgarity: 'the habit of judging human beings by standards having no necessary relation to their character'. To be found dwelling upon this vulgarity, absorbed in it, is like being found watching a dirty movie. It is no use telling people you were merely there as a detached observer in the age of

Deep Throat; in the case of fashion, too, the grubbiness rubs off all the same, upon scholars no less than novelists, socialites and gossip columnists. Seldom does a scholar, unlike a Balzac or a Gogol, treat fashion as an essential ingredient of history. Instead, he treats it as comic relief, usually set apart from the narrative in an archly written chapter with a coy title such as 'Bumpkins and Brummels; from Country Fair to Mayfair'.

Fashion in our own time is a more complex subject than it has ever been, and a more revealing one, I think. Which brings me back finally to Funky Chic and the Age of Egalitarianism. Fashion in our time, after all, is a much more devious, sly and convoluted business than anything that was ever dreamed of at Versailles. At Versailles, where Louis XIV was installed in suites full of silver furniture later melted down to finance a war – at Versailles one could scarcely be *too* obvious. Versailles was above all the City of the Rich. Hundreds of well-to-do or upward-hustling families had quarters there. The only proper way to move about the place was in sedan chairs borne by hackmen with straining trapezii. Anytime a notable of high wattage gave a party there would be a sedan-chair traffic jam of a half-hour or more outside his entry way as the true and original jeunesse dorée, in actual golden threads and golden slippers, waited to make the proper drop-dead entrance. One has only to compare such a scene with any involving the golden youth of our own day. I recommend to anyone interested in the subject the long block, or concourse, in New Haven, Connecticut, where Elm Street, York Street and Dixwell Avenue all come together. This is near the heart of Yale University. Twenty years ago, at Elm and York, there was a concentration of men's custom tailoring shops that seemed to outnumber all the tailors on Fifth Avenue and Fifty-seventh Street put together. They were jammed in like pearls in a box. Yale was still the capital of collegiate smart dressing. Yale was, after all, the place where the *jeunesse dorée* of America were being groomed, in every sense of the word, to inherit the world; the world, of course, being Wall Street and Madison Avenue. Five out of every seven Yale undergraduates could tell whether the button-down Oxford-cloth shirt you had on was from Fenn-Feinstein, J. Press or Brooks Brothers with a single glance at your shirt front; Fenn-Feinstein: plain breast pocket, J. Press: breast pocket with buttoned flap, Brooks Brothers: no pocket at all. Today J. Press is still hanging in there, but the rest of the heavenly host has shipped out. Today a sane businessman would sooner open a souvlaki takeout counter at Elm and York than a tailor shop, for reasons any fool could determine at a glance. On the other side of the grand concourse, lollygagging up against the Rexall and the Yale Co-op, are the new Sons of Eli. They are from the same families as before, averaging about $37,500 gross income per annum among the non-scholarship students. But there is nobody out there checking out breast pockets or jacket vents or any of the rest of it. The unvarying style at Yale today is best described as Late Army Surplus. Danny's Army & Navy enters Heaven! Sons in Levi's, break through the line! that is the sign we hail! Visible at Elm and York today are more olive-green ponchos, clodhoppers and parachute boots, leaky-dye blue turtlenecks, pea jackets, ski hats, long-distance trucker warms, sheepherder's coats, fisherman's slickers, down-home tenant-farmer bib overalls, coal-stoker strap undershirts, fringed cowpoke jerkins, strike-hall blue workshirts, lumberjack plaids, forest ranger mackinaws, Australian bushrider mackintoshes, Cong sandles, bike leathers, more jeans, jeans, jeans, jeans, more prole gear of every description than you ever saw or read of in a hundred novels by Jack London, Jack Conroy, Maxin Gorky, Clara Weatherwax and any who came before or after.

Of course, this happens to be precisely what America's most favored young men are wearing at every other major college in the country so that you scarcely detect the significance of it all until you look down to the opposite end of the concourse, to the north, where Dixwell Avenue comes in. Dixwell Avenue is the main drag of one of New Haven's black slums. There, on any likely corner, one can see congregations of young men the same age as the Yalies but ... from the bottom end of the great greased pole of life, as it were, from families whose gross incomes no one but the eligibility worker ever bothered to tote up. All the young aces and dudes are out there lollygagging around the front of Zombie's Get-Over Club ... wearing their two-tone patent Pyramids with the five-inch heels that swell out at the bottom to match the Art Deco plaid bell-bottom baggies they have on with the three-inch-deep elephant cuffs tapering upward toward the 'spray-can fit' in the seat, as it's known, and the peg-top waistband with self-covered buttons and the silk pattern-on-pattern Walt Frazier shirt, all of it surmounted by the midi-length leather piece with the welted waist-seam and the Prince Albert pockets and the black Pimpmobile hat with the four-inch turn-down brim and the six-inch pop-up crown with the golden chain-belt hatband ... and all of them, every ace, every dude, out there just *getting over* in the baddest possible way, baby, come to play and dressed to slay ... so that somehow the sons of the slums have become the Brummels and Gentlemen of Leisure, the true fashion plates of 1973, and the Sons of Eli dress like the working class of 1934 ...

... a style note which I mention not merely for the sake of irony. Just as Radical Chic among older people was a social fashion that ended up having a political impact – helping various radical causes – so did Funky Chic among well-to-do college students have a political impact: the opposite sort. So far as I know, no one has ever recorded the disruption that Funky Chic caused within the New Left. Remember the New Left? In 1968, 1969, and 1970 the term 'counter culture' was something that meant far more than it does today, i.e. it was more than merely the latest synonym for 'bohemian'. No, in those wild hot-bacon days on the campus 'counter culture' referred to what seemed to be a fast-riding unity of spirit among all the youth of the nation, black and white, a new consciousness (to use a favorite word from that time) that might possibly unite half the country – half the country was now under twenty-five years old, it was pointed out – under the banner of revolution or something not far from it. Yet at that very moment the youth of the country were becoming bitterly divided along lines of class and status for the first time. The more the New Left tried to merge them in a united front, the more chaotic and impossible the would-be coalition became.

Fashion was hardly one of the root causes of this division – the causes are another, longer story. But fashion was in many cases the cutting edge. Fashion provided symbolism that immediately, if unconsciously, red-flagged the factions to the differences that existed between them. And that was only half of it. Fashion also created hopeless emotional conflict where there was no ideological rift whatsoever.

In 1969 I went to San Francisco to do a story on the young militants who were rising up within the supposedly shockproof compound of Chinatown. I had heard of a sensational public meeting held by a group called the Wah Ching, who were described as a super-gang of young Chinese who had been born in Hong Kong, immigrated to the United States in the mid-1960s with their parents, couldn't speak English, couldn't get an education, couldn't get jobs – they had held a public meeting and threatened to burn down Chinatown, Watts-style. So I came on into Chinatown, cold, looking for the Wah Ching. Right away, on the street corners, I see groups of really fierce-looking young men. They've got miles of long black hair, down to the shoulders, black berets, black T-shirts, black chinos, dirty Levi's, combat boots. These must be the dread Wah Ching, I figured. So I worked up my nerve and started talking to some of them and right away I found out they were not the Wah Ching at all. They were a group known as the Red Guard, affiliated at that time with the Black Panthers. Not only that, they were not lower-class Hong-Kong born Chinese at all but American-born. They spoke English just like any other Americans; and most of them, by Chinatown standards at least, were middle-class. But they said they were allied with the Wah Ching and told of various heavy battles the Wah Ching were going to help them out in.

It took me about two weeks, but I finally arranged a meeting with one of the main leaders of the Wah Ching themselves. We were going to meet in a restaurant, and I arrived first and was sitting there going over all the political points I wanted to cover. Finally the man walks in—and I take one look and forget every political question on the list. He has on a pair of blue slacks, a matching blue turtleneck jersey with a blue shirt over it and a jacket with a leather body and great fluffy flannel sleeves, kind of like a suburban bowling jacket. This man does not add up. But mainly it's his hair. After all this ferocious long black hair I have been seeing in Chinatown—his is chopped off down to what is almost a parody of the old Chinatown ricebowl haircut. So the first magnificent question I heard myself blurting out was: 'What happened to your hair?'

There was no reason why he should, but he took the question seriously. He spoke a very broken English which I will not attempt to imitate, but the gist of what he said was this:

'We don't wear our hair like the hippies, we don't wear our hair like the Red Guards. We are not a part of the hippies, we are not a part of the Red Guard, we are not a part of anything. We are the Wah Ching. When we got to this country, those guys you were talking to out there, the ones who now call themselves the Red Guard, those same guys were calling us 'China Bugs' and beating up on us and pushing us around. But now we're unified, and we're the Wah Ching and nobody pushes us around. So now they come to us and tell us they are the Red Guard and they've got the message and Chairman Mao and the Red Book and all that. They'll give us the message and the direction, and we can be the muscle and the power on the street power and together we will fight the Establishment.

'Well, the hell with that. We don't need any ideological benefactors. Look at these guys. Look at these outfits they're wearing. They come around us having a good time playing poor and saying, "Hey, brother." Look at those berets – they think they're Fidel Castro coming out of the mountains. Look at the Can't-Bust-'Em overalls they got on, with the hairy gorilla emblem on the back and the combat boots and the olive green socks on you buy two-for-twenty-nine cents at the Army-Navy Store. They're having a good time playing poor, but we are the ones who have to *be* poor. So the hell with that and the hell with them.'

Here were two groups who were unified ideologically – who both wanted to fight the old clan establishment of Chinatown and the white establishment of San Francisco – and yet there we remained split along a sheerly dividing line, an instinctive status line, a line that might be described by the accursed word itself – fashion – at least in the meaning that René König brings to it in this book. This example could be multiplied endlessly, through every situation where the New Left tried to involve the youth of the working class or of the slums. There never was a 'counter culture' in the sense of any broad unity among the young – and this curious, uncomfortable matter of fashion played a part over and over. I never talked to a group of black militants, or Latin militants, for that matter, who didn't eventually comment derisively about the poorboy outfits their middle-class white student allies insisted on wearing or the way they tried to use black street argot, all the *mans* and *cats* and *babies* and *brothers* and *baddests*. From the very first fashion tipped them off to something that was not demonstrated on the level of logic until much later: namely, that most of the white New Lefters of the period 1968–70 were neither soldiers nor politicians but simply actors.

The tipoff was not the fact that the middle-class whites were dressing *down* in order to join their slum-bound brethren. The issue was not merely condescension. The tipoff was that when the whites dressed down, went Funky Chic, they did it without even bothering to look at what the brothers on the street were actually wearing. The New Left had a strictly old-fashioned conception of life on the streets, a romantic and nostalgic one somehow derived from literary images of *proletarian* life from before World War II or even World War I. A lot of the white college boys, for example, would go for those checked lumberjack shirts that are so heavy and woolly that you can wear them like a jacket. It was as if all the little lord byrons had a hopeless nostalgia for the proletariat of about 1910, the Miners with Dirty Faces era, and never mind the realities—because the realities were that by 1968 the real hard-core street youth in the slums were got into lumberjack shirts, Can't Bust 'Ems and Army surplus socks. They were into the James Brown look. They were into ruffled shirts and black belted leather pieces and bell-cuff herringbones, all that stuff, macking around, getting over, looking sharp . . . heading toward the high-heeled Pimpmobile *got to get over* look of Dixwell Avenue 1973. If you tried to put one of those lumpy mildew mothball lumberjack shirts on them – those aces . . . they'd *vomit*.

Yet Funky Chic survives. And the language of fashion is always worth listening to. For fashion, to put it most simply, is the code language of status. We are in an age when people will sooner confess their sexual secrets – much sooner, in many cases – than their status secrets, whether in the sense of longings and triumphs or humiliations and defeats. And yet we make broad status confessions every day in our response to fashion. No one – no one, that is, except the occasional fugitive or spy, such as Colonel Abel, who was willing to pose for years as a Low Rent photographer in a loft in Brooklyn – no one is able to resist that delicious itch to reveal his own picture of himself through fashion.

Goethe once noted that in the last year of his reign Louis

XVI took to sleeping on the floor beside his enormous royal bed, because he had begun to feel that the monarchy was an abomination. Down here on the floor he felt closer to the people. How very . . . funky . . . Well, I do not intend to try to set up any terrific historical analogy. Nevertheless, it demonstrates one thing: even when so miserable a fashion as Funky Chic crops up . . . it does, somehow, bear watching.

And now let us join Professor König as he . . . *gets it over*.

1 For and Against Fashion

There is no arguing with the fashion
William Graham Sumner

From time immemorial fashion and its sparkling role in human society has engaged the minds of philosophers of all kinds and of all nations. If we consider their pronouncements without bias we will find a striking difference in their evaluations that must give us food for thought. To some, fashion is a manifestation of evil, it represents everything that is damnable. To others it opens up, with all its new developments, new horizons, enriches and diversifies life and makes it more attractive; it also acts as a powerful stimulus to the economy, which to its opponents seems only an inducement to luxury and the soft life and eventually to moral decay. These two opinions allow of no transitions, no compromise; there are no possibilities of conciliation, only extreme and one-sided value judgements.

Thus the prophet Zephaniah threatens all those with damnation who 'ape outlandish fashions' (Zeph. i, 8). Isaiah is even more outspoken; at the same time – against his own will as it were – he paints a colourful picture of the accessories of a lady of fashion of his time (Isa. iii, 16–24):

Then the Lord said:
Because the women of Zion hold themselves high and walk with necks outstretched and wanton glances moving with mincing gait and jingling feet, the Lord will give the women of Zion bald heads, the Lord will strip the hair from their foreheads. In that day the Lord will take away all finery:

anklets, discs, crescents, pendants, bangles, coronets, headbands, armlets, necklaces, lockets, charms, signets, nose-rings, fine dresses, mantles, cloaks, flounced skirts, scarves of gauze, kerchiefs of linen, turbans, and flowing veils so instead of perfume you will have the stench of decay, and a rope in place of a girdle, baldness instead of hair elegantly coiled, a loin-cloth of sacking instead of a mantle and branding instead of beauty.

At the beginning of the eighteenth century the witty London physician, Bernard de Mandeville, in his *Fable of the Bees* delivered a diametrically opposed judgement on fashion that is representative of a great volume of similar sentiments:

> Their darling Folly, Fickleness
> in Dyet, Furniture and Dress,
> That strange ridic'lous Vice, was made
> The very Wheel that turn'd the Trade.
> Their Laws and Cloaths were equally
> Objects of Mutability;
> For, what was well done for a time,
> In half a Year became a Crime;
> Yet whilst they alter'd thus their Laws,
> Still finding and correcting Flaws,
> They mended by Inconstancy
> Faults, which no Prudence could foresee.

Certainly the radical confrontation of these two examples reveals various aspects not necessarily connected with fashion: the negation of the flesh and contempt for wealth in the one; an equally marked worldliness peppered with a few grains of irony deliberately calculated to shock the reader in the other. It is nevertheless obvious that these opposite judgements express much more than personal preferences and idiosyncrasies, a point which we must discuss in some detail.

The extent to which the ambiguous attitude of the public

towards fashion has been constant over thousands of years is altogether remarkable. Socrates spoke for all husbands when he rebuked his wife Xanthippe for refusing to conform to the general custom and carry his outer garment for him during a procession: 'You do not go out in order to see, but in order to be seen,' as Aelian tells us. With their narrow-minded refusal to adopt any features of the Athenians' style of life, the Spartans set an example for equally parochial critics of fashion, who two thousand years later were derided by Schiller and Goethe. Xenophobia and Puritanism have been with us for a long time. In Rome we find on the one hand the *arbiter elegantiarum* and on the other Horace, who in his odes and satires attacked the followers of fashion of his time and those who imitated Persian customs: '*Persicos odi, puer, adparatus.*' There was the same opposition at the Seleucid and Ptolemaic courts where the soldierly austerity of the diadochs was in great contrast to their late master, the ostentatious Alexander: they wore their simple field dress with soldiers' boots, chlamys, a simple cape, and the Macedonian hat instead of the luxurious Persian clothes.

Altogether, moral criticism and the criticism of fashion always go hand in hand. Thus Savonarola raged not only against the dissolute life in Rome and Florence in the fifteenth century, but also against jewellery and fashion. This did not, however, prevent him from preaching in a language which closely followed the new, aesthetically aware style of his age; sometimes fashion gets its revenge by dominating those who despise it. In sixteenth-century England, Roger Ascham, tutor of the future Queen Elizabeth I, attacked Italian fashions with unprecedented ferocity; in addition to political undertones that were hardly surprising during the struggle of the English reformers against the Church of Rome, this expressed strong anti-Italian sentiments which had their equivalent on the Continent in the anti-French prejudice of the Germans. Such attitudes are closely associated with the view that regards following the whims of fashion, moral corruption, and lasciviousness as synonymous. At the beginning of the seventeenth century Johann Michael Moscherosch launched out in voluble tirades against the Frenchification of the Germans; he was following faithfully in the footsteps of Abraham a Santa Clara, the hellfire preacher at the Imperial Court in Vienna. At the same time numerous guide books were published on courtly manners, with a very positive approach to fashion, although their authors, like all the classical scholars, warned against bad taste and excess. During the eighteenth century fashion in Germany became totally identified with French attitudes; Lessing was the most notable representative of this trend.

As late as the middle of the nineteenth century Friedrich Theodor Vischer took up the same subject with singular virulence and talked about fashion and cynicism in the same breath; cynicism in this context is synonymous with wantonness. What really incensed him was the fashion of the Second Empire in France, then entering the stage of its most refined elegance; he was particularly outraged by the '*cul de Paris*'. At the other extreme was the poet Baudelaire who explored with fine intellectual distinction the relation between art and fashion, and the brothers Edmond and Jules de Goncourt with their charming studies of women in the eighteenth century, while at the end of the nineteenth century a poet of the rank of Mallarmé did not shrink from actually becoming the editor of a fashion journal. These are only a few examples to which we could add many others. Again and again we find that concern with fashion results in two factions, uncompromising and irreconcilable. A pointed argument against Isaiah's diatribe is an observation we come across quite often during the nineteenth century: the feeling of being in harmony with fashion gives man a measure of security religion can never give him. Oscar Wilde was one of the chief proponents of this view.

Only a few decades ago the establishment of such an

1. Tanagra figure of a noble Greek lady in chiton and cloak (about 320 B.C.). *Historia photo*

2. Madame Grès, the great Paris couturière, at work. *Modebuch Verlagsgesellschaft, Zürich*

3. Egyptian dancers, about 1500 B.C.
Historia photo

4. Antique bikini, imperial villa in Sicily, Roman Empire
Staatsbibliothek Berlin

ambivalent and antithetical reaction would have been regarded more or less as a mere paradox, which could at best be used as a caution against any attempt of one-sided interpretation and against an underestimation of 'man and his contradictions'. But since the advent of psychoanalysis we have a much deeper understanding of these attitudes; nor do we any longer see them as simple differences or opposite views of our environment. In fact we know today that we must expect intense interest of society in the focal object or attitude whenever we encounter such rigid and irreconcilably opposed value judgements of public opinion. The Swiss psychiatrist Eugen Bleuler has coined the term 'ambivalence' for this phenomenon, a term adopted by Sigmund Freud as well as by psychoanalysis in general. The expression precisely describes the 'double values' of sentiment or attitude discussed here and indicates that a certain aspect of human experience has both a positive and a negative emotional side. Whereas the average person is able to weigh these various emotions against each other and somehow to balance them, the sick person leaves them to coexist in 'affective ambivalence'.

Now we do not wish to deal here with psychopathological phenomena no matter how interesting they may be; what we are concerned with is the behaviour of largely healthy people. But here, too, we may sometimes find this attitude of ambivalence as soon as we are confronted with behaviour patterns in which emotions and drives in the widest sense play a part. Society itself will then evolve an ambivalent attitude. As Freud says: 'At the root of every taboo, there must be a desire.' A certain desire is perhaps present in the subconscious, which is counteracted in the conscious by appropriate rules of social behaviour. This is the 'ambivalent relation' proper. When we apply it to our present case we can claim that to the criticism of and attacks against fashion that have constantly recurred throughout known history, there is, on the other hand, a corresponding secret need for it, strong enough to break every sanction and to overcome every conceivable obstacle time and again.

We must not be surprised that here society interferes with an attitude which, to begin with, we feel is a purely personal matter; after all, our entire behavioural spectrum is determined by socio-cultural factors. When we consider the many mandates and taboos controlling the structure of everyday drives such as hunger and sex, the innumerable value judgements that decide what is right or wrong or what is decent and acceptable in word, manner of speech and writing, in omission, commission, or avoidance, we find again and again our social environment influencing our behaviour.

Our daily lives are without doubt hedged in by an abundance of social rules and standards which surround them like fortress walls; they not only force us into a certain direction but also tell us expressly how to do the right thing. These rules and precepts are the stricter the more important a certain kind of behaviour is, or appears to be, to society. Sexual taboos are thus definitive in the extreme and almost religiously unconditional; as far as some customs are concerned it might merely be suggested to us that we should observe them; a certain amount of latitude is left to personal tact and taste.

The fact that the approach to fashion can be extremely critical implies that here, too, society is deeply concerned with the behaviour of its members and their activities. It clearly means that fashion is not merely a superficial – decorative or disfiguring – feature of life, but also that it constitutes an important regulator and means of expression within the community of man. Man's self-expression in society, his self-assertion – inward as well as outward – and also his social classification and competitive distinction from his fellow man have depended, ever since he formed a community, to a truly astonishing extent on that mysterious force we call simply fashion.

Why is so much importance accorded to a seemingly harmless phenomenon such as fashion that we should mention it in the same breath as religious taboos? Are we not wildly exaggerating its significance? If we resort to the arguments of psychoanalysis, obviously not because the very aversion and outrage fashion has again and again created and of which we have mentioned a few examples is striking proof that we are confronted here by a powerful social force. Now everybody will readily agree that human dress, which appears to be the primary object of the development of fashion, is of some importance especially in northern latitudes as a protection against the rigours of the climate. On the other hand this importance cannot be all that great because a large section of mankind manages without clothes, or with very few. One would not really expect a phenomenon that fluctuates within such a wide range to arouse such strong interest. The question we have to answer, however, is whether we may confine ourselves purely to the matter of dress or concede that fashion goes far beyond it.

In his book *Totem and Taboo* (first published in 1912) Sigmund Freud has the following observations to offer on this point:

> An unconscious impulse need not have arisen at the point where it makes its appearance; it may arise from some quite other region and have applied originally to quite other persons and connections; it may have reached the place at which it attracts our attention through the mechanism of 'displacement'. Owing, moreover, to the indestructibility and insusceptibility to correction which are attributes of unconscious processes, it may have survived from very early times to which it was appropriate into later times and circumstances in which its manifestations are bound to seem strange. These are no more than hints, but if they were attentively developed their importance for our understanding of the growth of civilization would become apparent.[1]

[1] Authorized translation by James Strachey, Routledge and Kegan Paul, 1950.

In other words, even if fashion seems to be associated initially with dress only, interest may largely have been attracted to it from elsewhere, for instance from eroticism. This reveals a truly instinctive root of fashion and sheds a completely different light on the controversy about it. It shows this controversy to be an expression of those social sanctions that have always opposed any manifestations of the sex urge. For this reason also J. C. Flugel, an important supporter of psychoanalysis, stresses in his *Psychology of Dress* (first published in 1930) that our attitude to dress has been ambivalent from the very beginning, the principal confrontation being between emphasis on adornment on the one hand, and modesty or respectability on the other. Indeed, dress attempts to balance two contradictory aims: it emphasizes our attractions and at the same time supports our modesty. But both aims spring from the common root of the sex urge, acknowledged in one, denied in the other. This is in agreement with the previously mentioned ambiguousness of public opinion concerning fashion. The ambivalent attitude to dress is obviously a result of displacement. We are already stressing here that this displacement mechanism is by no means confined to dress, but has entered many other facets of civilization; so too its origins must be sought outside dress. Fashion, in the course of its development in the history of mankind, has made more and more aspects of civilization serve its purpose, so that it now appears to be one of the most important formative principles of modern mass society. Here we find again an ambivalence of attitude in the positive or negative valuation of 'consumption' which represents, as it were, the broadest background to the capacity of fashion to vary.

2 Fashion-oriented Behaviour — Content and Form

It is not our intention to trace the development of fashion back to the beginnings of human records when man was emerging from the grey dawn of prehistory. That is a task that has been tackled many times before. What we want to do is limit ourselves to the investigation of the special relationship, already outlined, of fashion to human society (strictly, our approach is sociological). We shall have to illuminate this relationship from two angles: firstly, the psychological and social conditions from the time fashion-oriented attitudes came into being to the development of dress, and secondly, from this to the further questions of economic and social development.

This implies that we shall largely ignore the 'contents' of fashion, which are never the same in any culture, at any level of development, in the various eras, and in the different economic and political systems; any information on this aspect is readily obtainable from any history of fashion or moral history. We are mainly concentrating on the principles that act on the root of fashion, and their social functions and ramifications. This obviously does not mean that we shall not occasionally look in passing at the history of our subject, but the purpose of this will be merely to present examples. At the end of our book we shall point out certain basic variations of fashion in the present day that have given it a considerably enlarged importance within the modern economic system, and above all have freed it from its exclusive association with the upper classes; in short, have radically democratized it. But first we shall have to describe a number of different styles in which fashion has spread, and which are derived from the basic structure of fashion-oriented behaviour; in the course of history they have undergone progressively more drastic transformations, which eventually make fashion appear inseparably bound up with the general development of the economic society. We shall look at the history of fashion in the proper sense only when the subject has become topical beyond the structural problems.

In tracing this development, we shall, however, have to proceed in several clearly discrete steps. To begin with we must obviously look at the direct outward form of fashion; it will appear to us above all as an important, very short-term law of movement of social dynamism. This is also the aspect of fashion that first catches the observer's eye and to which most students of fashion have confined their research. But as the centuries-old confrontation with this image of fashion has appeared to us as the manifestation of other, more profound forces, which through the mechanism of displacement become evident in their outward form, we must now trace the roots of these forces in a second series of investigations. Our third step will seek to reveal the ramifications through which fashion spreads beyond the design of dress, and this will naturally bring us into more intimate contact with the history of fashion. Here too, however, we must pay more attention to the structural aspects than to the abundance of the various outward forms, so that we shall largely confine ourselves to describing the development of what we shall call the various styles of the spread of fashion.

We therefore distinguish between the socio-psychological, structural form of fashion as a social regulator in its own right and its various and forever variable contents. This also implies that we take fashion completely seriously as an independent social institution. It has – as will soon become apparent – its own place in the total economy of regulated patterns of social behaviour, which also explains the sometimes truly elemental force with which it breaks down every resistance.

This approach to fashion also means that, unlike the many fashion writers in the daily papers, journals, illustrated weeklies and magazines, we do not want to pronounce judgement on various fashions. As we have already pointed out, our real intention is to analyse the 'system of fashion'. This also means keeping a certain distance from the fashion of the day; for if one occupies oneself with the fashion of the day one will succumb to it and automatically be caught in the dialectical whirlpool of its infinite variations. Roland Barthes has recently shown how the topical fashion writer continuously develops a new language to circumscribe whatever is new in his field; one of the important functions of this new language is to consign yesterday's fashion to oblivion. The fashion analyst's task, on the other hand, is different: he does not want to forget but on the contrary to present fashion as a whole from the earliest beginnings of mankind down to the present day in order to be able to identify its laws. He will achieve this aim only if he keeps his distance. The analyst of fashion is not obliged to be fashionable himself.

3 The All-embracing Reality of Fashion

We must destroy here and now the widely held prejudice that fashion is only concerned with the outer cover of man in dress, jewellery, and ornaments. Since it is a general social institution it affects and shapes man as a whole. Hence those descriptions of fashion that interpret it simply as the study or history of dress are inadequate. In reality fashion is a universal, formative principle in civilization, capable of affecting and transforming not only the human body but also all its modes of expression. This is why its cultural-creative force must not be underestimated, although it is identical neither with culture as such nor with the special manifestation we call 'style'. Manifestations such as the Renaissance, Baroque, Rococo, Neo-classicism, Sturm und Drang, Romantic Age, Naturalism, Impressionism, Expressionism, New Functionalism, Surrealism, etc. are much more far-reaching ways of shaping civilization, pervading all its expressions and thereby also requiring a longer period of time for their complete evolution and inner adaptation; conversely, they then display a powerful persistence as cultural forms, which also show a tendency towards uniformity. We call these manifestations styles, in contrast to fashions which introduce the exact opposite – continual change – into the picture; this can be confined within a given framework, when it will be a variation on a certain theme; thus many roughly similar fashions enliven one and the same style.

Again, fashion can suddenly break out of such a framework,

which raises the question of how far it will be accepted. If it is, it may happen that after the swings of the pendulum have died away a new permanent form will be created. It is true that many cultural forms have sprung from fashion, but many alleged styles have with hindsight shown themselves to be mere fashions. Nevertheless there is, both in culture and in style, an element that is essentially lacking in fashion of permanence and persistence during long historical periods. In fashion the dynamic component is predominant so that its cultural significance will be particularly prominent when sudden spasms of movement begin to transform a traditional system. We shall see later that fashion is distinguished by a very fast rhythm of development. But this does not by any means preclude the possibility that, in some conditions and after prolonged experimenting, a fashion or a related sequence of fashions with a restricted range of variation can give rise to a new style. We would even hazard the guess that all styles have started as fashions, but after more or less extensive experiments have developed or as it were have 'crystallized' into a permanent form.

Crystallization or condensation phenomena of this kind, however, are found not only in the products of culture that 'bid the fleeting moment stay' but also in the social regulating systems where, in the opposition of fashion and custom, the tension between fashion and style is repeated. Exactly as before, here too it appears that no custom is completely rigid, but permits a whole range of fashionable deviations of short duration and narrow latitude. In what conditions deviations from a custom are acceptable, and for how long, is also laid down; this legitimate deviation applies particularly to the upper classes. One could in fact say that a custom (like a style) will have reached its limit when it no longer permits any variants and stubbornly lays down a rigid canon. The fashion usually begins its sallies into new territories, becoming progressively bolder, until one day the old system collapses, in fact mostly quite unnoticed. Whether a new custom crystallizes from the many fashions is another question that only the historian can answer; the man on the scene is too closely wedded to the present to be a good judge. But the contrast between historian and contemporary must not be exaggerated. Only too often a detailed study will reveal that a seemingly ancient custom traced to its beginnings may really have started as a fashion craze not so very long ago. It is, incidentally, an old experience that short-lived fashions are so conspicuous that they blot out, as it were, the recollection of their predecessors.

These and similar phenomena, however, are possible only because fashion is a social regulating system in its own right and differs from other regulating systems (such as those of habit, custom, convention, morality, and the law) only in degree, not in essence. Even during its short life it can therefore develop into definitive enduring forms. This is shown, incidentally, in the economic sector by the persistent efforts of the manufacturer of some 'novelties' to give his products the character of staple consumer goods, in demand not only during a single season but for many years and even decades, until a definite 'monopoly of opinion' is established. Special efforts, such as publicity campaigns, will usually be made to achieve this situation. At the other end of the spectrum we have the fads: minor manifestations of fashion, adopted for their very originality but usually dropped again after a short time, eccentricities of fashion, crazes that are here today and gone tomorrow.

We have long since learned to correlate style and fashion and to pave the way for a quantitative representation of their respective developments, as was done above all by the well-known American anthropologist, A. L. Kroeber (1919, 1940). In spite of the apparent unpredictability and complete arbitrariness of annual fashions it has been shown that they fit into relatively regular secular rhythms of sometimes long duration which can extend across several centuries, that is, constitute real characteristics of style. These long-term changes, for example in the length or width of a dress, the extent and level of the waist, the width and depth of the neckline, are interrupted by minor fluctuations, short-term manifestations whose directions appear to the contemporary observer to deviate sometimes very considerably from the general trend. In fact the regularities of the long-term development quite outweigh these minor fluctuations. From this objective viewpoint it becomes evident that there are periods in which these impulses for change become more frequent, for example during wars and revolutions; this usually initiates a change in the direction of the general development.

Kroeber was able to show beyond doubt that women's dresses reached a minimum of width around 1811 and 1926, and a maximum around 1749 and 1860. This represents 'wave lengths' of 115 and 111 years respectively. For other measurements (length of the dress, level and width of the waist, width and depth of the neckline) other periods of fluctuation apply; this is not surprising since the variability of the various formal components of dress is oriented to different dimensions of civilization and as a result some of these components develop independently from one another. From the long-term waves we distinguish fluctuations of fashion that represent true 'deviations' from the general line of style. It is easy to outline periods of major and of minor frequency of deviations. It is most astonishing to realize the extent to which these periods of fashion development coincide with certain historical developments and correspondingly are reinforced by other historical impulses of change. Kroeber found strong fluctuations before 1800 which subsided until 1815 and increased again up to about 1835. The era of the Revolution and the Directory was most unstable, that of the Empire relatively stationary and the period following it at first again very unstable until it found a new balance. Another period of change began in about 1900, becoming particularly marked in some fields in about 1911,

1920, 1923, 1930 and ending in about 1933. The question arises as to how the situation developed since 1935 and whether the fluctuations of fashion during and after the Second World War recurred in the same rhythm as Kroeber has demonstrated so strikingly for the preceding centuries. It would be worth while to take up Kroeber's investigations again and to continue them for the period from 1935 to 1970 on the basis of the criteria he used.

The 1970s show without doubt an instability similar to that during the French revolution and during the 1920s. Skirts had been becoming shorter and shorter for many years up to Mary Quant's mini-skirt, and then sudden reactions followed with the floor-length maxi-skirt and the corresponding maxi-coat worn sometimes with the old mini, sometimes with longer dresses. Occasionally a decision based on indecision produced the so-called 'midi-look', calf-length dresses. This is a typical expedient, the sort of thing that makes people who cannot decide between a red and a white wine for their meal choose rosé. The female trouser suit, on the other hand, strikes us as an interesting new creation, perhaps grown from a typical 'displacement' whereby a new line that contrasts with the mini but departs from the form of the skirt has been evolved. Apart from the need for contrast there was perhaps the fact that a surfeit of panties and sometimes rather ungainly thighs were revealed by wearers of the mini-skirt. We therefore believe that in the trouser suit a longer-lasting fashion variant has been created (we would not like to say the same about the maxi-dress). A similar 'displacement' is evident in the recent hot pants, a modification of the old shorts, which avoid some of the disadvantages of the mini-skirt without changing the line.

It is at any rate a cardinal point that it is not revolutions, wars, and socio-cultural instability as such that create certain fashions (long or short dresses) but rather that they challenge the existing style. They develop divergent tendencies, subversive and centrifugal movements.

This opens up a fresh insight into the depth dimension of fashion. Even when a custom or a style is firmly established there is always a variation range for deviant behaviour. Only when the deviations exceed certain limits will they create problems in that they will soon encounter increasing pressure and resistance from the community, which seeks to enforce the observance of traditional customs or styles. This contest between deviation and resistance has always been a central feature of social life. It ranges between the two extremes of absolute conformity and an equally absolute arbitrariness and rejection of all rules.

The peculiarity of change in fashion is founded on the fact that the deviation from the hitherto observed and binding custom becomes as much a law as the regular behaviour. Fashion change thus confronts style as a constant temptation or a constant challenge to break out of its constricting circle. It is the experience of this relationship that arouses strong passions in those who belittle fashion and in the same breath anathematize it – which makes one wonder how the degree of aggressiveness of these critics can be reconciled with the alleged triviality of fashion-oriented behaviour. But this is precisely the problem: the laws of style and custom can fit into the framework of historico-social progress only under the constant threat of deviation, for it is this that opens up the dimension of creative spontaneity in which life is ever new and different.

Thus, fashion as a regulator in its own right becomes a pacemaker of social change, in the course of which customs and the tradition of style reach their end and new possibilities are opened up. The grave-digger assumes the role of a midwife during the birth of a new order and a new style. The possibility of regular behaviour is unthinkable without the continuous willingness to deviate, for without this the rule itself would, in the long run, lose its point and degenerate into a concept of simple habit. It is exactly here that the special circumstances of war and revolution cited by Kroeber gain their real significance, because under their influence the tendencies to deviation, always present, become intensified.

Fashion cannot therefore be understood in the light of a certain object with which it is particularly closely associated, such as dress. On the contrary, it refers to a specific behaviour pattern in the most varied situations and in relation to the most varied objects. This peculiar attitude has up to now been characterized by its very short-term change, and in fact *by a brevity of term that is not purely arbitrary but socially regulated and determined*, i.e. by a regularly recurring, more or less far-reaching change of our entire behaviour that is expected of us by our social environment. This creates on the one hand the possibility that enduring habits could develop from the suddenly transformed behaviour; on the other hand, this transformation may last less on some, longer on other occasions. It is, after all, obvious that a fashion in costume jewellery must change more rapidly than in furniture, more rapidly in the cut of a dress or its colour than in its general outline (long or short, narrow or wide skirt), more rapidly in film-stars or a popular hero of a novel than in certain fundamental tenets and values of a political allegiance, more rapidly in interior décor and style than in architecture and town planning. The object with which it is associated is thus without doubt important for the persistence of a fashion in time, but not for fashion-oriented behaviour as such.

This reveals, incidentally, a fundamental peculiarity of fashion: the social regulating system of fashion does not simply join other regulating systems, such as the already-mentioned customs, habits, etiquette, conventions, morality, and laws, as a system of particularly short-term fluctuating changes; even within itself, fashion splits into behaviour patterns of varying degrees of persistence. One has only to think of the American 'gadget' and the British 'craze'. Their relation to fashion is the same as that of fashion to style or to custom. For within the framework of any fashion we can discern currents that are even more short-term, often lasting only a few weeks, which are called poses, rages, fads. These are frequently characterized by the fact that they are *a priori* confined to certain groups of society – the well-to-do, the young, those interested in the arts or the stage, special groups such as students, sportsmen, soldiers, airmen, sailors, young workers, etc. Such a fad is recognized most easily by its superficiality and usual lack of influence on general attitudes. The Beatle haircut of our days is a good example. It is obvious that this applies also to literary and artistic fashions. The craze or rage as well as the fad is also associated with a certain irrational exaggeration which is naturally confined to the few people who can indulge (economically or morally) in such whims. It does not apply to all otherwise dedicated followers of the fashion of the day. But that such a staggering of short- and longer-term fads, crazes and true fashions is possible within the structure of fashion is yet another indication that, in spite of a life that is by definition short, fashion must have the rudiments of a more long-term and far-reaching effect; it is this quality that establishes its relation to style and custom, in no matter how many other features it may differ from them.

From this point of view the realm of fashion becomes all-embracing. Nothing that enters the sphere of human activities can escape its power. Like a thief in the night it intrudes everywhere, ultimately casting its spell even over those that had never the slightest intention of yielding to it. Shakespeare described it in a servants' dialogue in *Much Ado About Nothing* (III, 3):

> *Borachio*: Seest thou not, I say, what a deformed thief this fashion is, how giddily 'a turns about all the hot bloods between fourteen and five and thirty, sometimes fashioning them like Pharaoh's soldiers in the reechy painting, sometime

like god Bel's priests in the old church window, sometime like the shaven Hercules in the smirched worm-eaten tapestry where his codpiece seems as massy as his club?
Conrade: All this I see, and I see that the fashion wears out more apparel than the man. But art not thou thyself giddy with the fashion too, that thou hast shifted out of thy tale into telling me of the fashion?

The human body, in posture and gait, in movement and expression, is completely formed by fashion. Even health and sickness are subject to it. Sicknesses become fashionable just as do the physicians that cure them. In about 1830 every artist and snob was posing as a consumptive; at the *fin de siècle* the pose of depravity was 'in' even among conventional and ordinary people. During the twentieth century the pendulum has swung to the other extreme; we have the fashion of ostentatious health, of the straight and upright posture, the suntanned skin of both men and women (in contrast with our grandmothers' pallor of the harem). If it is impossible to obtain a natural suntan, powders, lotions, and artificial sunray treatment are called in. Associated with this is the fashion for an athletic and hardy appearance, again in both men and women, coupled with an expression of fatuously beaming simplicity, seen at its most typical in the Hollywood 'keep smiling' pose, the 'glamour' of American politicians and public figures, and the pin-up girl. The 'smart' appearance of the perfectly groomed modern businessman is as much part of it as the deliberately slovenly appearance of the hippie.

Under this influence our men's fashion has experienced a radical change and shoulders have become broader in contrast to our grandfathers' 'Gothically' drooping ones. For a time, when chest measurements were not sufficient padding was used to create the impression of real boxer's shoulders. Modern man wears his grandfather's epaulettes inside the lining of his jacket, where, although demilitarized, they continue to fulfil

5. Noblewoman, Middle Ages (note the protruding abdomen). *Staatsbibliothek Berlin*

6. Jost Amman: Woman, Strasbourg 1577 (from a book of folk costumes) *Staatsbibliothek Berlin*

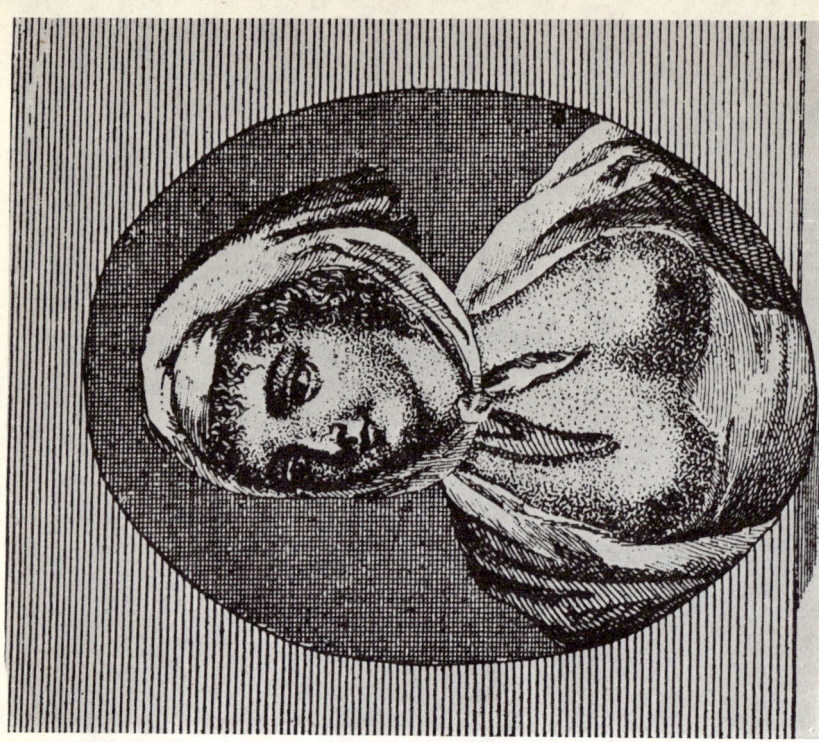

7. An old document dealing with the topless question (That bare breasts are a great temptation of sinful desires is proved for

8. Topless fashion, young woman, about 1750. *Archive Gerstenberg*

The All-embracing Reality of Fashion 49

their function discreetly. Jackets have become looser, trousers wider; the waistcoat has been replaced by the football jersey, even by those who would never be seen dead on a football ground. Under these influences our posture has become generally more relaxed, less stiff and strait-jacketed, our gait less mincing, the movements of our arms and hands more sweeping and less constricted – especially since the disappearance of the starched shirt front, the stiff collar and the pretentiously rustling starched cuffs. This new trend towards greater mobility has persisted even since the old waistcoat reappeared under the influence of a romanticizing movement; the fluctuation of the width of men's trousers today is passing through a phase similar to that of the length of women's skirts.

What applies to the elementary postures applies equally to all natural body adornments. The Romans already experienced changing fashions not only in the wearing of a beard, but also in the varying shapes of beard. Sometimes the vogue was the clean-shaven face of the Greek ephebe, at others the curled beard of the Farnese Hercules, or the austere schoolmaster's beard of the Stoic. The ancient Egyptians saw fashion changes in hair ornaments and hair-styles; primitive inhabitants of the African bush share this experience, and prehistoric man (as numerous finds of hairpins and hairslides give evidence) was no exception. There are even occasions when beard fashions or hair-styles were expressions of fashionable political currents or of the adherence to certain philosophies, such as the hair and beard style of the liberals and progressives of the nineteenth century, the Emperor Francis-Joseph beard, the upturned twirled ends of the Kaiser's moustache, the Garibaldi beard in Italy, the Balbo beard during the Fascist regime there, as well as the brushed-up, stove-pipe-shaped hair-styles of young Italians around 1925 at the time of the 'squadristi' and of futurism.

More recently a narrow, curling beard growing from the ear over the cheekbone to the chin or simply proliferating wildly become the label of the existentialists: a fashion originating in the Paris of the Left Bank but which spread almost everywhere. Its female counterpart was the tight-fitting, dark jersey, closely modelling the bust, combined with corduroy slacks and loose-hanging hair, a look first launched by Juliette Greco. Make-up or its absence depends just as much on fashion as the laced or unconstricted bust of young and more mature women, as the mincing gait of the 'lady' or the long, camel-like stride of the American bobby-soxer.

We ask ourselves in vain where the line is to be drawn between the natural and the artificial. Indeed, such a difference does not exist where fashion is concerned. Everything is a prescribed pose, a set attitude, convention. Even the nudist disporting himself in his birthday suit follows the bidding of fashion no less than the lady at the turn of the century who, with a huge, bobbing cartwheel hat, parasol, and frilly ankle-length bathing costume, sought at the seaside to protect herself from the noxious influence of the sun. We shall presently show how mistaken it is to speak of one fashion as being more 'natural' than the other, of 'progress' in fashion, or of 'over-refinement'. All this springs from a perspective which applies alien yardsticks to the prevailing fashion. Fashion is what it is, grown entirely from its own roots: it recognizes neither artifice nor nature, but only its own all-embracing law.

This law has no limits. It begins in the modelling and posture of the body and extends to all the occupations, attitudes, ideas and interests of man. If the slim line is fashionable all girls and women appear as slim as young saplings; but as soon as fuller figures are 'in' they will change their attitude from one day to the next with the same force of conviction and disarming self-assurance. But both men and women also think, feel, and desire what fashion commands, so that in the end a single, regular thread is established, running from the colour of the tie to the political affiliation, to the emotion, to the most intimate expression of the soul. Small wonder, then, that the products of our environment, too, follow this dictatorial command: ashtrays and architecture, tubular furniture and garden layout, railway locomotives, car bodies and the design of our cities and cultivated countryside change as the merry-go-round of fashion turns and turns. And if someone cared to argue that surely a high mountain landscape is not subject to fashion, we would have to tell him that as a mountaineer he would most certainly be extremely susceptible to fashion. For what is the attraction of the highest rockface, the steepest ridge, if nobody climbs it or walks on it, as nobody did for thousands of years and nobody will perhaps do again in the far distant, unknown future? We know at any rate that Petrarch, with his ascent of Mont Ventoux, started a strong current of fashion which gradually engulfed ever larger sections of society with the new feeling of affinity with nature. To realize that fashion is really limitless we only have to appreciate that it is not confined to concrete matter but is a part of our fashion-oriented behaviour.

Fashion is indeed an unacknowledged world power. Even in the great clamour of world history it guides man with a soft yet insistent voice. But again and again we forget its all-pervading presence and stare transfixed at the great public figures of the day who sometimes have themselves been carried to the top by the currents of fashion. Fashion is thus perhaps more powerful than all the other powers on this earth. We are therefore fully justified today in speaking of fashions in literature and art, of more or less short-term currents even of a political nature which often transform the entire behaviour of man.

These phenomena need not, however, be confined to the role of liberating man from the strait jacket of an outworn past as they so often do in the battle between the generations. On the contrary, they may very well develop into new elements of style. But we must also add at this point that in view of the extraordinary abundance of experiences that occupy the minds of fashion-oriented people today the number of faulty solutions that reach a dead end and can only enjoy an ephemeral existence must correspondingly increase. Nor is anybody in a position to predict which of the current fashions are pregnant with the elements of tomorrow's styles. With the general intensification of life the number of dead or dead-end fashions that life creates at every turn also increases, only for the most part to be just as quickly discarded. And so the cultural inventory of our age looks only too often like a dismal rubbish dump of the whims of yesterday's fashion, succumbed to for a day and abruptly discarded with the creation of new forms. But the effort of undertaking ceaseless new beginnings can never discourage us for the human richness of continual self-renewal carries within itself its own justification. Thus fashion has become a world power that is now an integral part of our existence.

4 Change and Stability

This realization, however, raises with some urgency the question of the outward characteristics of fashion-oriented behaviour. We repeat that this is not a matter of tracing the various historical contents of fashion nor the objects with which it is mainly concerned. According to our previous arguments this approach is already barred to us. What we have to attempt is to reveal the structural form of fashion-oriented behaviour in isolation, that is, the mechanism fashion obeys, the characteristic attitudes and behaviour patterns that occur whenever fashion is involved. This attempt must begin with a formal analysis as the starting-point for further inquiries. Even now it can be assumed that a large number of driving forces must support fashion if it really is to wield the universal power we have just claimed for it.

But a danger arises of which we must be aware from the outset, especially when we study the literature on fashion. This danger consists in citing, after the demonstration of the mechanism of fashion, only a single principle in explanation, with the result that different viewpoints will be taken up and there will be interminable controversy. Such a controversy is pointless simply because a phenomenon as universal as fashion can quite clearly never be explained in terms of a single root without its interpretation suffering severely. We are thus driven to using a large number of viewpoints to explain the mechanism of fashion and the structure of fashion-oriented behaviour.

This is done on the assumption of a special feature of fashion which we call its 'versatility'. We might even include from the outset the notion that fashion can occasionally appear self-contradictory. We must stress once again that we shall begin with the outward aspect and from there trace the roots and real driving forces of fashion. We shall then observe its further 'displacements' across the field of dress in the narrower sense to the larger one of civilization and the economy.

The only basic characteristic of fashion-oriented behaviour we have outlined so far was an important feature of its outward appearance – the short-term nature of fashion change. At the same time we indicated that this change is subject to a certain social control. This gives us access to a definition of fashion-oriented behaviour offered by the Dutchman S. R. Steinmetz: 'Fashion is a periodic change of style of a more or less compulsory character.' This is a purely descriptive statement, deliberately and rightly avoiding any attempt at an explanation. It merely insists that fashion is a matter not only of a purely factual, but also of a socially commanded change. At the same time we obtain already an insight into a first fundamental contradiction of fashion, a contradiction which has frequently struck observers: the second part of the sentence does not quite appear to tally with the first. To understand this assertion we must be clear about one point: the second part of the definition does not just refer to a 'compulsion' to *change* (which in itself would not yet indicate a contradiction, but in a way merely underlines the first point); in fact, this compulsion applies equally to the behaviour at each newly reached stylistic stage. For at this moment the obligatory change of style acquires yet another, completely different, character: after the compulsion to change, to abandon the traditional form, it leads to a compulsion to adaptation, indeed to the closest possible assimilation to the new kind of style. Adaptation is expected in the special form of assimilation; in other words, after the completion of the abrupt change the obligation to carry out the change also dictates a standing still or stabilization within the framework of the new situation, and a close adaptation to the new conditions. This applies at least for a certain period until a renewed compulsion to a change in fashion occurs. But a measure of consistency remains: the demand for a sudden change must, with rare exceptions, be based on a certain consensus regarding its direction. This attitude is also evident in the advice never to be the first in a change of fashion, or the last: the first 'kicks over the traces', and 'the devil takes the hindmost', and both more or less lay themselves open to ridicule, one because he is in too great a hurry and displays excessive zeal, the other because of his obstinacy.

All this does not yet tell us much about the short or long term of fashion change; we must first find out about the length of the period of adaptation. But we do know something about the suddenness of the process. We shall in due course appreciate the reasons for the short duration of fashions. It will at any rate have become clear that fashion is mainly time-oriented and therefore part of the dynamic laws of society. Furthermore, the problem of adaptation to a completed change seems to be of paramount importance in the development of fashions; this adaptation is also unique in that it must not occur 'at any time', but at the (fashionably) right moment.

This is not the point at issue now; we are concerned with a much simpler problem. In fashion, abrupt change and an equally abrupt tendency to stabilize, both demanding adaptation, constitute a paradoxical situation. But this tendency to stabilize is not a mere accident, a result of loss of energy, or fatigue after an intense effort; it has a decisive function in the realization of the aims of fashion because it always occurs during that period when the accomplished change becomes a fashion in its own right, that is, gains the upper hand quite irrespectively of whether this fashion crystallizes into a custom or a style. In other words, it passes into the new dimension of extended duration and ceases to be quite specifically fashionable in the accepted sense. Without doubt there are impulses of change that do not develop into true fashions but for the most varied reasons rapidly disappear into limbo, possibly even after a brilliant display. These are the real 'miscarriages of fashion' as we might call them; they also include the already mentioned fashionable trivia, the whims and fads.

For a fashion to assert itself a certain amount of time is necessary, if only until it becomes conspicuous, its characteristics are realized, and the public have adapted their behaviour to it, which occasionally entails far-reaching changes in attitudes. Since social processes are not mechanical but depend largely on the thoughts, feelings, intentions and, above all, the perceptions of the individual members of society, a certain 'signal period' regularly elapses before the public have absorbed and grasped new events and correlated them with their current complex of ideas. Only then will it become possible to perform real acts of adaptation and to assimilate individual behaviour to that of one's fellow men. Thus change is necessarily and directly accompanied by a period of stability until the sense of the change of fashion has been grasped, interpreted, and finally digested.

In addition, the fashion stimuli must first pass through the filter of the hitherto dominant behaviour patterns and customs, and this also takes a certain amount of time. The surprise of the novelty and sometimes the eccentricity of what is offered must first wear off; this is occasionally followed by an experimental phase of the fashion. A striking example is the period immediately after the Second World War, when the New Look in women's fashion with its early nineteenth-century associations was at first worn with the sporty, low heels fashionable during the war – a plainly unsatisfactory combination. By the time the matching high heel was introduced the fashion of the classical New Look had already been replaced. With the mini-skirt, on the other hand, high heels look out of proportion. Thus new types of boot were designed, made of crinkled leather and other materials, and reaching above the knee. This experimental attitude became more pronounced with the arrival of the maxi-coat: suddenly knee breeches or knickerbockers were worn under it with or without high boots; sometimes the mini-skirt persisted, or long trousers were worn; and intermediate forms had long slits in the back or side of the coats up to the hip, exposing the thigh. Something similar happens when the impulses for a change of fashion break completely with tradition without sufficient justification in the general social conditions. This results in the already-mentioned abortive fashions.

Beyond these examples, however, we must record that fashion does not exhaust itself in aimless and uninhibited change, but combines change and stability. Moreover, this stability is not an accidental phenomenon but indeed the decisive factor, since we cannot speak of a fashion when only a few people have begun suddenly to act, dress, behave, and think differently. Only when large numbers of people have been affected by the change will a fashion in the narrow sense of the word have been created. But once this has happened, we cannot get away from the 'signal period' which, it must be added, has completely different effects on the different generations, sexes, social classes (upper and lower), and regions (town and country).

It will thus be appreciated that the spread of fashion is closely dependent on the existence of a 'scene', a stage on which the novelties are displayed. Ostentation and demonstration are essential features of fashion; and the ways in which the fashions spread also change with the various forms of ostentation and demonstration. Fashion does not and cannot exist in seclusion; it wants the world for its stage. It needs to see and to be seen; it has an indisputable trait of exhibitionism. In ancient times the market place and the agora played the part of the stage for fashion; Horace, taking a stroll, became aware of the peculiarities of his environment (*'Ibam forte via sacra, nescio quid meditans . . .*'). In the Middle Ages and the Renaissance up to the end of the eighteenth century the court took the place of the agora of Ancient Greece; it occupied a more or less central position. In the Feudal Age proper on the continent with its many courts large and small there existed quite a considerable number of local and regional fashions, often inspired by local folk costumes or, conversely, inspiring them. Certain courts radiated a special splendour quite early on – the Provençal courts of the eleventh to the thirteenth centuries for instance, or the court of Burgundy which, under Philip the Good and Charles the Bold, influenced the whole of Europe with the fashions of Burgundy. However the future belonged not to these regional civilizations but to the great central courts of the Age of Absolutism in France, England, and Spain which, on an exalted plane, were exposed to the view of their respective countries and ultimately of the whole of Europe. Their function in the spread of fashions is therefore extremely important; we shall see how they constitute the very climax of a certain mode by which fashion was spread.

There were other periods in which the theatre, as a social occasion, regularly attracted large crowds and from about the time of the Restoration (baroque) it was used for the display of fashion. To begin with, all forms of baroque festive occasions, such as processions, coronations, receptions, tournaments (Richard Alewyn), were repeated on the stage, until finally, along with the advent of the 'bourgeois tragedy', the middle classes became interested in the theatre and used it to display their wealth and the new fashions. With this went theatrical shows of every kind, such as had always been customary in the Italian city states whether at the reception of foreign emissaries or spectacular dramas like the burning of Savonarola. The salon in France performed the same function from the eighteenth century on, although it was characterized by greater intimacy.

In all these cases we have a very clear concentration of

fashion display in an exactly defined meeting place; but another change occurred in this respect in the nineteenth century. Although some of the courts survived, their influence progressively waned; there were a few exceptions: those of the Empress Eugenie's Second Empire, and of the Prince of Wales, later Edward VII. The theatre, too, in spite of Richard Wagner's *Bayreuth* and later in spite of Max Reinhardt, lost more and more of its 'festive' character and became finally a mere place for entertainment and education. But now the European cities and capitals, above all Paris, were claiming increasing prominence as centres of intense and sustained social activity, roles they have never to this day relinquished. Their function with regard to fashion can be easily outlined: 'to see and to be seen', on the boulevards and corsos, during festive occasions of all kinds, at the theatre, opera, variety show, during horse races, regattas and other sports events. In short, fashion disports itself in public to the maximum extent, and accordingly makes very early and direct use of all mass media (daily papers, journals, illustrated weeklies, film, television) to parade before the eyes of the whole country and ultimately the whole world. It shows itself everywhere, it is seen, thought about, understood, taken up, modified and, finally, perpetuated. Compared with this giant stage the 'specialized' and 'professional' fashion shows are without doubt less significant, and are important only to those whose ambition it is to be pioneers of fashion: they have no direct appeal to the public at large.

But these were later developments which we shall presently study in greater depth. We return now to events which, especially within the framework of life at court, carried the already very powerful, inherent influence of the courts on the spread of fashions to a climax that has probably never been surpassed. These were the great court festivities on the occasion of a coronation, an engagement, or a wedding, and even the lesser ones marking a newly concluded alliance or merely a hunting party. Here, not only was a sometimes unprecedented extravagance ostentatiously displayed within the course of a few days or even hours but, at the same time, the current fashion was developed to aesthetic perfection during weeks and months of preparation, and the kind of, and reason for, the display studied in the greatest detail; there were many rehearsals and the impact of the performance was raised to its maximum.

Such festivals, religious and secular, generated the strongest fashion impulses from the Middle Ages on, quite apart from the fact that they were the true causes of rivalry for prestige among the upper classes, a subject to which we shall return. Important too were the festivals of the middle-class and urban civilization of the Middle Ages and the Renaissance which regularly united many people from all the feudal territories, above all at the great fair-centres; visitors not only made merry and bought their wares at the fair but also displayed, saw, and finally accepted, the latest fashions. These festivals were used by great architects for the opening of new festival halls, palaces and staterooms and they stimulated painters. We thus have magnificent representations of the contemporary fashions of kings, princes, and noblemen, and of patricians who were striving not to be outshone by this display.

The long history of these festivals indicates that they satisfy a profound need of social man. The medieval fairs evolved from the occasions in Ancient Greece when people came together from all over the country to sanctuaries such as Delphi and Olympia; the great festivals held from the Middle Ages on were modelled on basic elements of the Roman triumphal processions. Indeed a similar kind of procession often became the central event of these festivals. Later, the actual parade developed into a theatrical performance which finally assumed the form of ballet; performances also arose in which only a small part of the public took an active part while the rest respectfully admired the pageantry from their windows or from the street. This was a subject for painters such as

Agostino Carracci of Bologna and later Nicolas Poussin in France.

Apart from these developments, which are supremely significant in the history of civilization, the importance of such festive occasions for the spread of fashion consisted mainly in the fact that they acted like a time-lapse mechanism for the signal period. The entire range of novelties was displayed within a relatively short time to large crowds concentrated in the smallest possible space. It is therefore not surprising that it could often be proved that some fashions began at such a festival. The time-lapse effect compressed into a few days processes that otherwise required often months or years for their development. If it coincided with a sudden fashion change, such a festive occasion caused the fixation of the fashion concerned in the imagination of large crowds of people, who lost no time adopting what they saw and establishing a new habit.

Now the basic feature of fashion as the cause not only of a change in style but also of a far-reaching movement of adaptation contributes to its potentially becoming a habit, a usage, even a custom. In spite of its unpredictable nature fashion is thus a behaviour pattern in line with habit, usage, and customs. Special conditions must perhaps be met if a fashion is to result in lasting behaviour but at this stage it is enough to realize that it can happen. We can, however, assume that in a change in fashion a certain proportion of the public must always take the lead, to be followed at a certain interval by the rest during a longer-drawn-out process of adaptation and assimilation.

Lastly we must point out that the pressure exerted by the environment in favour of adaptation and assimilation springs from the same source as that of custom or any other social standards of behaviour. For every deviation from the new line of fashion eventually provokes a slight social disapproval. Naturally this disapproval will not be very noticeable so long as fashion has not crystallized into a custom. It nevertheless exists in so far as the adherents of the fashion of yesterday or the day before are regarded as a little antiquated, behind the times, not 'with it'. Subjectively this is experienced as an awareness of standing out too much from one's surroundings, possibly of being slightly ridiculous. This awareness will be the stronger the more susceptible a group is to the changing impulses of fashion (we shall demonstrate later that this susceptibility to fashion is by no means equally strong in all social circles), and generally the more rigid the rules of behaviour are in a group. Very individual reactions, too, can be observed here, depending, for instance, on how far a person has become integrated into a group. It is obvious that a newcomer will seek to adapt himself more quickly (this is the reason for the comical haste with which the typical *'nouveau riche'* follow every, even the slightest, whim of fashion: they constantly fear that they will 'miss the boat'), but there may also be a profoundly personal insecurity, which to those suffering from it makes even the slightest disapproval of society intolerable; they always have to race ahead, so to speak, in a hectic, restless urge towards change which ultimately threatens them with a real loss of personality. These are the hysterics of fashion, the true fashion snobs.

We thus have a long scale of attitudes towards fashion extending from those who must be 'with it' at all costs to those who are almost completely unaffected by it. Of interest here are, above all, those leading a precarious existence and those living on the periphery of society, because they reveal most clearly the pressures fashion exerts towards adaptation. It is generally known that the French emigrants after 1789, the *ci-devants*, affected extremely exaggerated fashions, thereby often incurring the animosity of the indigenous population; the same applies to immigrants and generally to groups that are not yet fully accepted by the existing community and hope to narrow the gap by a particularly scrupulous observance of the fashion. Fashionable behaviour thus becomes a means to social advancement; we find, for instance, certain groups in the 'new' middle classes of the twentieth century, above all the white-collar workers, far more susceptible to the whims of fashion than the old bourgeois classes. The same applies to young workers. We must add to these all the groups on the periphery of society, the 'twilight world' and the 'underworld' of adventurers and impostors and those uncertain of their status such as the famous Teddy Boy. Typical in this respect is the behaviour of the Westernized administrative and business *élites* of the so-called 'underdeveloped' countries of the Near and Far East, Central and South America and the new countries of Africa. They are today the champions of a somewhat flashy elegance, always striving to beat their rivals by a short head. But they forget all too easily that whereas one principle of fashion decrees never to be too late, its essential opposite demands that one should not be too early either. Their behaviour here resembles that of adolescents who, too, like to kick over the traces in this respect; in our view this is a symptom of the regulating power of fashion, which itself occasionally creates absurdities.

A recent tenet of sociology of 'relative under-privilege' and the 'control group' allows us to deepen the analysis of the behaviour just described. Relative underprivilege is the disadvantage at which a person finds himself when members of other groups with whom he identifies himself acquire a certain 'status' as a social 'reward' from which he is himself excluded. The resultant feeling of being snubbed, accompanied by strong reactions of resentment, can create not only collective depression, but conversely lead to the exaggeration of certain fashions. The difficulty of reference to 'control groups' consists in the fact that those involved are continuously exposed to contradictory compulsive forces from the group to which they belong by reason of their origin on the one hand, and on the other, from the group of which they are not yet members, but to whose membership they aspire, so that the latter becomes the control group for the entire behaviour. This schizophrenic attitude emerges above all in the situation of social advance and is comparable in some respects with that of the snob.

After the impulse of fashion change has had its effect we find at any rate a subsequent strong urge towards uniform behaviour. This 'uniformity tendency' succeeds in inducing the members of a relatively homogeneous group to adopt a uniform general behaviour. By a fashion that has become uniform members of this group can now recognize one another; this creates a vague feeling of satisfaction and security. But there can never be a complete adaptation in any given large society. For firstly, every society includes innumerable different groups of very different behaviour patterns and correspondingly very different ways of reacting to fashion. In addition, members of each group enjoy a certain latitude, also determined by convention, within which they may personally modify the behaviour pattern that their milieu demands or follows. Complete uniformity is met only in rare, extreme cases and even then usually applies only to a single aspect: we think of the functionally determined uniform of the military, which by no means rules out civilian differences. This is also why completely uniform masses are so exceedingly rare; because with the numerical increase of a group the opportunities of a whole range of possibilities dividing it according to certain characteristics also increases.

Although the pressure of adaptation and assimilation exerted by fashion is relatively weak because the sanctions fashion is able to impose on those who fail to observe its decrees are comparatively vague, its formative power must not be underestimated. For who can, in the long run, tolerate the mocking smiles or undisguised ridicule of those he comes into contact with, quite apart from the fact that the use of fashionable products or the observance of fashionable behaviour is suggested to him the more forcefully the more a fashion asserts itself. Certainly he may resist this pressure for a while (there are indeed entire strata or parts of society that do this regularly). Certainly he may modify the new features for his own use. But sooner or later he will succumb – even feeling as he does so a certain satisfaction.

We must nevertheless not forget those who, for some reason or other, try to offer resistance to fashion. But even this resistance is not free from fashionable influences in so far as it may become fashionable among some groups and cliques not to follow fashion for a certain period. This produces a fashionable counter-effect, which may be triggered by the fact that some group, looked down upon by certain other groups otherwise leading the fashion, accepts a single fashion trend, with the immediate result that the fashion leaders reject it. This happens often when some fashions become universal. When, for instance, domestic servants, about fifty years ago, began to wear the same hats as their mistresses, large sectors of the wealthier strata of society abolished the hat. It was a long time before the ladies' hat gained a new status which, however, profoundly differs from the one it occupied before the First World War. Today the old status persists only among the lower-middle and the upper working classes. We shall discuss other forms of anti-fashion later.

5 Roots and Branches

We have so far offered only a purely descriptive definition of fashion-oriented behaviour and deliberately refrained from any attempt at explanation. But we have to carry our investigations farther in order to find the mainspring of the universal power of fashion. It is a strange quality of fashion that makes it appear more and more important the longer it engages our attention. It begins, as it were, at the outer shell of man and object, but finally presents itself as a universal formative principle of human society. We hope to substantiate this claim with the arguments that follow but want to emphasize again that we shall constantly bear the versatility of fashion in mind and accordingly try to avoid at all costs concentrating on only one line of explanation. Quite apart from the fact that the original drives and roots of fashion originate at all possible levels of the psyche from where they have been 'displaced' so that they became modes of dressing, it is noticeable in the specifically social sphere, too, that various impulses, which need not always be in harmony, are simultaneously at work in the development of fashion. Only thus will it become clear that fashion can affect innumerable vital manifestations of man, that its ramifications are noticeable everywhere.

It could of course be said (and it has indeed been said) that only in our modern consumer society has fashion achieved the overpowering significance we ascribe to it. Past periods going back to early antiquity, even to pre-history, witnessed expressions of fashion, but then they were invariably confined to the upper classes, that is, to a negligible minority compared with which the great mass of the population was strongly tradition-bound, altering its way of life only in terms of centuries. The proletariat thus displayed a tendency to evolve a traditional mode of dress as a form, for instance, of folk costume, or a more or less standardized and uniform mode of outward behaviour by which the members of a clearly defined group recognized one another. One could, on the other hand, claim that the increasingly fast-changing way of life of all (or at least very many) people constitutes a phenomenon typical of the present time: fashion would then be determined largely by its being simply 'modern'.

If we adopted this last argument we would not only be moving in a circle but we would also be led to claim that fashion is a behaviour pattern whose general spread occurred only at a precise stage in history. Anything earlier would at best be only a preliminary form of fashion, possibly a mere abnormality, limited furthermore to certain clearly definable and, in addition, very restricted groups. In a word, the assumption would be that fashion is purely historical growth without any deeper roots.

If fashion grew, in fact, only from certain historical premisses, it would indeed be the purely surface phenomenon that it is often regarded as, and nobody could ever be made to understand why it has such an uncanny power that man can hardly escape from it. We are therefore induced to search beyond the doubtlessly existing historical factors which today favour the spread of fashion among ever-widening sections of the population for other roots more deeply anchored in human nature. Without such roots the fateful, indeed tyrannical power of fashion would be beyond explanation. This does certainly not mean that fashion could be understood without any reference to history; we shall demonstrate the decisive historical elements in the modern consumer society later. But we must roughly redefine the relationship between anthropological (general human) and historical facts by exposing special historical conditions that favour the unhampered development of fashion. It can then be readily understood why the quality of fashion-oriented behaviour, the violence with which it asserts itself, largely points to more permanent roots than could be provided by a historically transient social and economic situation.

Such a sweeping statement at once raises a very obvious question: are we not running the risk of exaggerating the significance of fashion beyond all bounds? If the question is approached on such simple terms the answer must of course be yes. But it is not at all our aim to trace fashion-oriented behaviour exclusively to certain general and constant conditions in the depth of the human soul. All that is meant is that fashion 'overlies' basic psychological and social conditions which, incidentally, branch out into quite a large number of completely different phenomena. But when we say fashion overlies general, basic human conditions we imply something very important. It means no more and no less than that fashion is on no account merely a peripheral or superficial phenomenon of society but that, with its roots in certain basic anthropological, psychological and sociological conditions, it is really capable of becoming an elementary force of social developments. The extent and depth of fashion and of fashion-oriented behaviour also decides the range of its effects.

6 Fashion-oriented Behaviour in Animals and Children

In one way fashion is always becoming something new and different. But it persistently claims that it represents the true solution and completion of a special task, that it would therefore have to continue after the sudden change and to influence a maximum number of people who would lay themselves open to ridicule if they did not follow its commands. Fashion thus seems to include a loose strand, a trait of irrationality, levity, indeed frivolity, adventure, and superficiality that cannot be pinpointed. At the same time it expresses an inherent need and exerts a specific compulsion, both of which can be intensified until they assume the role of fate. A French quotation represents this quality most aptly: '*La mode est la fille du hasard et la mére des grandes tragédies.*' Fashion is the daughter of chance and the mother of great tragedies when, for instance, products already on the market are rejected by the potential customer because they do not answer his fashionable wishes and expectations.

How can we interpret this contradiction?

Here we have already achieved a first refinement of our claim that fashion is versatile, which also implies that it consists of many layers. For the apparent contradiction between change and stability is resolved once we realize that fashion is based simultaneously on a deep and on a surface layer of human nature. In a nutshell, man has a deeply rooted urge to be superficial and capricious.

How deeply rooted this urge is may be proved by the very fact that we can speak of genuine fashions even in the games of animals. It has, for instance, been observed that anthropoid apes will, one day, be completely absorbed by a game and will persist with it until, at a completely irrational moment, they will drop it and no inducement will make them take it up again; they will then change over to another game. When we remember the previously mentioned definition of fashion-oriented behaviour we shall find a striking affinity with the behaviour described. The same phenomena can, incidentally, be observed in the children's nursery.

Even if these and similar phenomena are merely spontaneous changes of behaviour without any social rule the analogy with the alternation in fashion between change and stability is striking enough. The playful change of behaviour patterns, all of which display a tendency to persist for a limited time, seems to occur not only in human adults but even in some animals and certainly in children. In addition, a surprising uniformity exists in the attitude of several individuals, which can almost be called assimilation. The modern animal psychologists even speak of a 'ritualization' of behaviour, in which certain movements, in the course of phylogenesis, lose their true, original function and become purely symbolic 'gestures' (Konrad Lorenz). They will then have the inevitability of instinctive actions. We are therefore completely justified in speaking of the preformation of a certain trait of fashion-oriented behaviour in animals or children. This demonstrates another aspect of this phenomenon most clearly: the compulsiveness of fashion occasionally has an almost mechanical side, hence the derogatory secondary meaning of the term 'uniformity', which denotes something of the flock or herd instinct. Now the behaviour of the herd does not (or not yet) constitute social behaviour. When a herd of wild animals flees from an approaching danger at a warning signal from the leader, this action alone cannot yet be considered a social reaction, although it is a uniform behaviour of a number of individuals. Naturally a relationship exists between the leader and the other animals; but its character is not specifically social. By its behaviour the leader triggers the flight instinct. In addition, every animal reacts individually to an external stimulus which could be supplied equally well by a completely different source (not necessarily by the leader). The reaction differs little from that of many people in the street opening their umbrellas at the same time in response to a sudden downpour.

All the same, we cannot reject this example out of hand when we consider the behaviour of children. For it is possible to note something similar in the 'dressing-up' games of children. Up to the age of two and a half years they never play games 'together' (that is, in the strict sense socially), but only 'side by side'; nevertheless, a relationship certainly exists of stimulus and reaction between the individual children; but the character of such a relationship too, is strictly not yet social. In children's games a specifically social impulse appears only later.

Without entering into discussions on animal and child psychology we can assume that the behaviour of animals and children occasionally resembles extremely closely fashion-oriented behaviour with its sudden change and subsequent stabilization. Although this provides insufficient reason to speak of definite 'germinal forms' of fashion one can, in view of the widespread occurrence of this behaviour among animals and children, readily assume without denying the existence of profound differences that such a behaviour may be transmitted in other fields of psychological development. For elementary behaviour patterns can very easily undergo a transformation and, above all, reinterpretation as soon as they are dominated by 'higher' psychological processes. It is most significant that even beyond the layer of specifically social behaviour we encounter certain patterns of reaction which in some respects appear to represent a preliminary form of fashion-oriented behaviour. That they nevertheless differ from it is already shown by the strong compulsion in children to repeat actions and, above all, by the strongly impulsive character of their behaviour. Even if an almost mechanically stupid reaction – really a snowball effect – often appears to predominate in fashion-oriented behaviour, the true social relations as distinct from those of purely reacting to stimuli will be clearly revealed even in the simplest cases. For beside the automatism of the uniform behaviour of large crowds there always exists a definite play of motivations, absent in both animals and small children. This applies no matter how primitive the motivations, according to the notion 'one has to behave like the others because it is the thing to do'.

We nevertheless cannot be indifferent to the fact that such a very sudden change of behaviour with a subsequent tendency towards inertia occurs beyond the layer of true social behaviour already in animals and small children within certain situations. After all, this phenomenon shows us how deeply rooted certain highly developed behaviour patterns can be in life in general. This establishes a definite gradient where behaviour patterns of totally different dimensions begin. This rudimentary preformation allows us to predict without difficulty that such higher behaviour patterns must grow and develop with a special intensity. Even the smile as a form of expression of a most highly differentiated character has its impulsive physiological precursor; but this in no way contradicts the fact that the social form of the smile has become a language in its own right, regulated by social rules and conventions. But the smile would certainly not have spread with such uniformity among the whole of mankind and persisted with such stubbornness and strength without a primitive form of stimulus as its basis. This does not preclude the occurrence in the dimension of civilization of completely different impulses, absent in all the lower strata.

Of particular significance for fashion appear to us the physical structures or inborn movement patterns, called triggers by animal psychologists, that provoke a response in the observer or recipient of certain signals. Such triggers exist according to Konrad Lorenz in all sensory fields; they may be visual, aural, or olfactory and play a decisive part in the capture of prey and the recognition of offspring or of the sex partner. Especially in this last respect the association with fashion is most obvious, so that a few words about these new discoveries in animal psychology are appropriate. At the same time the vital significance of these mechanisms becomes clear.

Experiments with dummies were conducted to find out what combination of characteristics a trigger must have to produce the strongest possible effect; the result was astonishing in that it showed how little resemblance the dummy need bear to the natural object to have the intended effect on the eye. A robin, for instance, would attack a tiny bunch of rust-coloured feathers as vigorously as a real rival. This led to further experiments in which the dummies and their characteristics were progressively 'dismantled'. It was shown that each isolated characteristic is capable of acting as a trigger, although its effect is less powerful. It was therefore concluded that the effect of a dummy corresponds to the sum of the individual stimuli of its various characteristics: the 'stimulus summation phenomenon'. This seems to us to be closely related to the phenomenon of fashion.

These characteristics, acknowledged with certain inborn reactions, in animals constitute combinations that cannot be further subdivided. Such 'communication characteristics' also play quite a special role in persons who respond to some expressive movements of other persons. We find Lorenz's claim highly significant that it is the visual triggers that are most important to man, who is a visual type. They represent the keys to certain reactions. It is immensely instructive to learn that especially the optically effective movements of this kind are 'mimically exaggerated', that is, 'their optically effective features are almost grotesquely underlined and overemphasized, very often with the formation of certain characteristics of shape and colour enhancing the optical effect'. We also speak here of 'symbolic motions', again with an obvious reference to the previously mentioned ritualization of behaviour.

Konrad Lorenz has proved that all this cannot merely indicate a distant relation of similar phenomena; he has himself established the connection to fashion, which he calls a 'super-optimum dummy' because it emphasizes certain indicators of the hormonal sex functions and of full sexual adequacy, for instance with excessively applied make-up. Here we have without doubt a powerful reason for the use of paint, which plays such a prominent part in fashion, a technique almost as old as mankind according to the evidence of paint pots found in the oldest known civilizations. Primitive cosmetics covered the dyeing and styling of hair, painting of the lips, teeth, eyes and eyebrows, painting and tattooing of the cheeks, breasts and abdomen, the back and especially the buttocks, which were frequently enlarged with feathers and other ornaments; sometimes one went to the length of 'breeding' steatopygous women, who were considered sexually particularly attractive. Since the sexual challenge contained in the colourful emphasis on certain sexual characteristics aims in the last resort at sexual union, which is its true justification, the role of these triggers in the preservation of the human race could not be revealed more clearly. Naturally, other senses, too, are mobilized for this purpose, such as hearing, where the different sound of the male and female voice has a decisive effect, or smell, whose significance in the attraction of the sexes cannot be overestimated and has been confirmed in the production of a wide range of scents since the dawn of human existence. The general impression of fashion-oriented behaviour is itself a phenomenon of stimulus summation in the strict sense, in which innumerable signs, each with its separate effect, by their combination make an unusually strong impression, and appropriately orient the behaviour of those to whom these signals are addressed. In the last resort, fashion-oriented behaviour is thus embedded in the complex necessary for the preservation of the species, and the urge to dress up as the fashion decrees accordingly acts with the same elementary force as any other urge serving the continuation of the human race.

7 Novelty, Curiosity and the New Look

When we look at fashion from this angle, we shall see clearly that certain roots which cannot be associated with fashion and are therefore more persistent continue to exert an influence on it. Although the contents of fashion are always a manifestation of their epoch and pass with it, its structural form as a special kind of the previously described controlled behaviour incorporates certain constants which decide initially what fashion is. In this it is similar to many other social phenomena, such as the family, which, like any transient elements, would probably have disappeared long ago but for the fact that some of its roots go deep down into human nature. If we take fashion seriously we must accept that fashion-oriented behaviour as such is not a fashionable phenomenon even if its individual contents change continually.

Hitherto, the sudden change of behaviour appeared to be an important basic characteristic of fashion. This sudden change opens up, in some corner of our existence, something new, which seeks to assert itself with a certain compulsive force. In this respect the New Look assumes the role of fate for fashion and fashion-oriented behaviour. This implies that man's receptiveness for anything new is among many other aspects in some way essential to fashion-oriented behaviour. If we disregard here all special forms in which new features may appear and concern ourselves solely with the conditions on which such behaviour is founded, we shall ultimately again be referred to the sphere of driving forces. Hence also the often repeated attempts to postulate in man a special 'urge towards innovation', a 'neophilia' that can express itself in the most varied ways.

If we trace the root of the stimulus that corresponds to such behaviour, we arrive at what a literal translation of the German term would describe as 'avidity for anything new' – curiosity. This is the complex of behaviour with which man acquaints himself with what is new to him. In so far as fashion with an abrupt change of behaviour always creates new contents, it, too, is based on such inquisitive behaviour. The striving after innovation indeed dominates man with elementary force ranging from behaviour patterns at the lowest level to the highest spheres of perception and a completely irrepressible desire for the radically new, for what has never been seen, never been heard before. The yearning for knowledge, sensationalism, religious visions 'to end all visions of heaven' and the passion which tears the veil from the statue at Sais are all part of that incomprehensible, insatiable quest for innovation, which also becomes evident in fashion-oriented behaviour.

Here, too, we must point out that we can observe certain precursors of inquisitive behaviour in some animals, and these have therefore been put in a class of their own. Here, however, the active range of new features is limited by the instincts. The more powerful these are the more limited becomes the field in which such new features can become visible. The more higher behaviour patterns occur, the more receptive will the creature be for the experience of innovation, the more intense accordingly will be its curiosity. In the face of the fundamental reliability of instinctive behaviour the occurrence of curiosity becomes the expression of a fundamental insecurity; this insecurity, however, is the price man has to pay for the overflowing richness of cultural life. Instinct confines itself to a world strictly limited to the species in which it operates. In the civilized world we must allow for the existence of an excess of driving force which can be directed towards anything that is in the widest possible sense a subject of experience. Here we recognize how elementary functions of the psyche trigger impulses which can spread across the entire civilization, without any need for an attempt to derive 'higher' from 'lower' forms. For the curiosity of man, which ultimately makes the world infinite, has little in common with the curiosity of a playful animal investigating everything within reach. The power that drives man to examine anything new, however, is rooted in the greatest depths of his existence. It certainly does not illuminate culture as such; but it does open up its wealth expressing itself in ever new forms. The end of curiosity would be reached only once all potentialities of life are completely exhausted.

When, for the moment, we look at only one side of fashion – the sudden change of behaviour – we can infer from what we have just said a permanent disposition for change, an unappeasable restlessness, a state of continuous expectation, merely waiting for the moment to change the old-established behaviour patterns. At what point in time this will in fact happen is on the whole beyond prediction, because this expectation after all represents a permanent willingness to change, which is activated by the weakest impulse. It is also because of this circumstance that external influences could become so important for fashion, since fashion picks up its ideas here there and everywhere as soon as the need for change has reached a certain urgency.

This is also what the trade speculates on when – first slowly and feeling its way cautiously, then with more and more determination – it begins to offer new wares once a fashion has lasted for some time. But this must by no means be interpreted in the sense that fashion is created by the fashion trade as is so often claimed. For in the absence of this readiness for fashion-oriented behaviour that creates a completely open-minded curious expectation, all inducements of the fashion trade would be in vain and fail to achieve any sudden changes in the behaviour of the public. It is precisely this elementary tendency towards fashion-oriented behaviour that offers the chance of success of such speculation by the trade. Such behaviour, however, is never created by the seasonal collections of the fashion trade. The form of fashion-oriented behaviour is thus the basis of the trade in every respect; only the contents can be determined by the trade – at least to a certain extent. An element of pure speculation therefore remains with every fashion collection: fashion-oriented behaviour is not only unpredictable as regards the moment of change, it is also selective and lets itself be guided by the most varied external influences. It often takes innumerable offers to persuade the fickle customers to rise to the bait, thereby lending current market value to the fashion products. It must, however, be admitted that the age of mass production with its immensely variable range of goods in all sectors favours a more frequent re-orientation of fashion. We must therefore be prepared for a general acceleration of fashion developments today compared with the past.

To this acceleration is added an enormous widening of the spectrum of fashion, of its 'collection' in the loosest sense. What happens is that more, different, and new objects become subject to the whim of fashion. This has the logical result of expanding the kaleidoscope of fashion combinations, which have long gone beyond the classical constellation of basic line accessories. Certainly this complicates matters in some respects; for ringing the changes on all the combinations of the infinite possibilities of variation in this spectrum of fashion may occasionally cover up a lack of imagination. This is particularly evident in those phases of fashion that derive their ideas from history and syncretistically combine elements of various origins. Nevertheless, what is genuinely new will sooner or later assert itself with a sudden push and thereby bring to an end what was a mere rearrangement of familiar elements. The true fashion is always *nouveauté*. The term 'novelty' acquires its irresistible appeal by indicating a step into the unknown. As a transition this entails the already mentioned experimental phase during which a process of selection and decision determines which of the new possibilities are ultimately adopted.

9. Frans Hals, Regents of St Elizabeth, 1641; classical example of middle-class men's fashion, in black cloth and white linen. *Staatsbibliothek Berlin*

10. (*Far left*) Women's fashion (about 1895), example of middle-class restraint. *Historia photo*

11. (*Left*) Women's fashion (1896), informal, colourful, imaginative style *Historia photo*

8 To See and to be Seen

Although a continuous transition exists between the simple curious behaviour and the yearning for the infinite, the *mal de l'infini* as the French call it, this statement must be couched in more concrete terms to acquire a specific meaning in the field of fashion. In other words, we now know what fashion has in common with other general cultural behaviour patterns; we do not yet know its specific features, we still have to inquire into the special direction of the spirit of curiosity that becomes active here.

We demonstrated at the beginning of this investigation both man's ambivalent approach to fashion and the underlying structure of the driving forces of fashion-oriented behaviour that associates it closely with eroticism. Indeed, curiosity, too, increases very strongly where sex is involved. This is an integral part of the basic dilemma of fashion, which has to choose between the display and emphasis of physical attraction, especially of the female sex, and the preservation of modesty. But this reveals very clearly the extent to which original driving forces can change under the influence of civilization, although we are in this context confining ourselves to the urge, which is of course of decisive importance to fashion, to see and to be seen. Sigmund Freud offers an interesting derivation for this phenomenon, too; he shows that the exhibitionist urge is originally auto-erotic, that is, refers to the subject's own body. The Goncourt Brothers gave a magnificent description of it in their novel *Manette Salomon*: the heroine freezes in front of the mirror in rapt contemplation of her own naked body. Only afterwards is the urge to see directed towards another body for comparison. In the end, this object, too, is abandoned and the urge to see turns towards a part of the subject's own body; at the same time the activity of looking is transformed into passivity and the establishment of a new goal, that of being seen. This also posits a new subject, to whom one shows oneself in order to be seen by him. Freud calls this relation, in which in spite of the 'drive transformation' and its reversal of activity to passivity the older, active direction of the drive persists beside the newer (passive) one, also ambivalent. We thus have on one side the tendency towards active visual contact, moving from the subject's own to someone else's body, that is from narcissism to fully developed eroticism, which perceives its visual object in the other body. On the other side the desire to be seen grows from the same erotic root; in its extreme form it can become open exhibitionism as Arthur Schnitzler shows in his novel *Fräulein Else*.

Inquisitive behaviour is thus here most intimately connected with the erotic root, whereas its specific form of expression is to be found in seeing and being seen. This also denotes that in spite of the clearly erotic condition of all fashion-oriented behaviour the satisfaction of the sex urge need not be included in it. On the contrary, one could even claim that nothing detracts the sex urge from its proper goal of the sexual union more than the play of eroticism in fashion, which with the mechanism of 'displacement' frequently expresses itself precisely where from a purely sexual aspect a vacuum exists.

We see this as a basic feature of the female form of eroticism, whereas the male in this respect is more direct and therefore often completely misunderstands the female play with the body and with everything used to cover as well as to uncover it. On the other hand, we must also stress that, besides the displacement and diversion of the erotic effect to dimensions that are not primarily sexual, the body itself occasionally appears quite frankly as an erotic object, whether through an ostentatious display of the erotic effect of the skin or of the secondary sexual characteristics such as the female breasts, or the display of certain limbs whose erotic significance has been familiar ever since dress in the true sense came into existence. Not only the arms, but above all the female legs belong to this category; they have therefore remained covered almost throughout the entire development of fashion. An important exception is the slits in the sides of the Chinese skirt which make use of the erotic attraction of the female knee hollow. In Europe the female leg has become uncovered up to the knee only in the twentieth century; this trend created for fashion an incomparable work of art in the silk stocking, which models the shape of the leg by enclosing it in a most delicate tissue and adds the highlights of silk, rayon, or nylon to the natural beauty of the bare skin. The revolution started by the display of the female leg has already been long forgotten. In its initial stages it was far more intense than when the mini-skirt revealed the thigh. Nevertheless the basic situation, in which this display serves the ends of eroticism, has not changed and the outcry this has provoked is precisely in line with the general aversion so often shown to fashion. 'Showing a leg' in India is even today considered the worst moral lapse a woman can commit.

We said before with Freud: 'At the root of every taboo there must be a desire.' The curiosity that leads to a continuous change in fashionable behaviour acts basically like the child's fantasy of the forbidden, makes the continuously changing female dress a constant source of fascination for the men, with the erotic element usually remaining quite unconscious. That it nevertheless exists is proved by the rantings of the outraged guardians of morality as well as by the compulsive and irresistible attraction of the forbidden, which has held mankind enthralled from the beginning of civilization.

9 Decoration and Distinction

Although curiosity admittedly plays an important role in the sudden change of behaviour, it is by no means the only factor responsible for this trend. In its urge and search for innovation life overreaches, transcends itself. It breaks out from the confined circle of its presence and explores the unusual, which is beyond the bounds of tradition, and thus moves from the present into the future. But variation and change need not be associated with self-exaggeration; the change is possible also within the framework of a self-sufficient existence, and began at the moment man picked up some object and attached it to his body for the purpose of decoration.

We do not ask here whether man is particularly prone to boredom so that, after he has become accustomed to everyday routine, tired, and dull, he simply longs for a change. We are inclined to think of boredom in terms of an outstanding product of civilization rather than a feature inherent in life itself, a feature still faced with the great tasks of orientation in view of the innumerable unexplored possibilities of human existence. But one can assume that the self-transformation through ornaments occurs quite spontaneously, which is all the more likely because ornaments have a double significance, as a transformation and enhancement of the person concerned in his own eyes, as well as a distinction from his fellow men. Thus the skilful hunter who has bagged a particularly beautiful bird will wear a feather in his hair. He thereby confirms his luck in his own eyes and to some degree prolongs his momentary and unique success; at the same time he tells the others of his achievement thereby gaining a distinction.

Decoration and distinction usually develop together, even if there are forms of distinction other than decoration. This common development is a feature of great importance in fashion. But the desire for decoration and distinction, too, has ramifications not only in fashion-oriented behaviour, but also in a large number of other behaviour patterns. To us they are relevant particularly because they include a spontaneous action, which deviates from the habitual and conventional. At the same time it provides a powerful stimulus to the rest to catch up with the leader; this introduces for the first time the factor of competition. But when we look around in history, we discover a strange phenomenon; it is true that decorations are worn spontaneously, but the manner in which they are worn will immediately assume permanent forms which sometimes persist unchanged for centuries. This applies irrespectively whether the decorations are durable or not; even grass, flowers, leaves, ropes, hair, pieces of fur, bones, teeth, shells, seeds, very simple wooden hoops, etc. can serve as fixed and permanent patterns for ornaments, which will then become socially and traditionally standardized. This shows that the original desire for adornment is in line with fashion in only one respect; in another it exhibits distinct style-forming elements, so that the periodicity of a change in style is somewhat less prominent in its oldest forms. The original forms of adornment are more closely related to folk costumes than to fashion. Both the forms of adornment and the ornaments therefore have a religious and magical significance. Both occasionally become as immutable as religious laws. This naturally did not prevent ornaments from becoming also subject to the changes of fashion in the course of development; but in the original appearance of the ornaments this is without doubt a relatively minor element.

In spite of this differentiation from fashion-oriented behaviour proper we do, however, find quite a number of indirect relations between the original desire for decoration as a distinction and for fashion. The British sociologist Herbert Spencer recognized at an early stage the extraordinary significance of trophies of all kinds in our complex of problems. Someone who, for instance, has slain an enemy in battle would wear certain parts of his victim's body as a record of his victory for all to see. Practically anything can be used for this purpose: the scalp, entire heads, limbs, bones, but also weapons, pieces of clothing and ornaments. Some of these objects were kept in the home, possibly to be proudly displayed on certain occasions; others were worn on the body, for instance teeth as pendants, or cheekbones as armlets. Thus the trophy, too, ultimately became an ornament; bones and other objects were often richly adorned usually with symbols of religious significance. It is this feature which, as we have already said, gave these forms of adornment a rigid and immutable character. We must on the other hand not forget that the kind and number of trophies a person acquired was completely accidental. Especially here, competition introduced the element of variation with the result that at least individuals wore sometimes more, sometimes fewer ornaments of various descriptions. Adornment thereby acquired yet another function, that of expressing wealth.

Ornaments as an expression of wealth have developed from all objects of acknowledged value. This does not mean that something has to be precious according to our standards; but it must be considered precious. This may concern any object occurring in a given civilization. If an item is not found in a certain territory it is on the whole not used as an ornament there, at least not for routine and everyday wear. But there are many exceptions from this rule: innumerable examples exist of materials imported from distant countries being used as distinctions for persons of high rank. This idea was contradicted by the early theory that primitive man confined himself to small local markets. But the discovery of the ancient civilizations in the East shows how certain materials used for adornment travelled over enormous distances; the most famous example is perhaps the presence of cowri shells from the Indian Ocean in prehistoric European tombs. The Red Indians in what is now Arizona and New Mexico obtained obsidian from the region of Yellowstone Park, corals from the Pacific coast and later from Japan, and, at the end of the nineteenth century, turquoise through traders from Iran. Numerous other examples could be quoted, such as the export of silk from China since the third century B.C. as far as the Mediterranean region. Owing to their rarity these objects from distant sources were usually hoarded in treasure houses and proudly displayed only on special occasions.

The close association of these elementary manifestations of fashion with a great variety of other phenomena becomes obvious here, particularly when we consider decoration as an expression of wealth: occasionally this connection between decoration and wealth can become so close that articles of decoration and money become all but indistinguishable in what is called 'ornamental money'. This also reveals the fact that the original function of money differed from today's in that it circulated rarely if at all and sometimes remained with its owner in the form of ornaments. The custom persists even today among many peoples; gold coins are sewn to the bodice, or worn on necklaces and bracelets, or as pendants on men's watch chains, where they have the same function of distinction as the wild boar's tusks for the successful hunter. Such forms of adornment may occasionally remain unchanged for centuries. This leads to an important realization which is not always sufficiently appreciated. Even the most primitive man knew innumerable forms of decoration, but we must not deduce from this that fashion is as old as mankind itself. For this aesthetic elaboration of the human body, although it occurred spontaneously, did not periodically change. Thus the forms of ornaments of prehistoric peoples were extraordinarily constant. We must, however, point out that even in these primitive civilizations an occasional fashion change did take place, caused, for instance, by certain eminent personalities (warriors, chieftains, princes, priests, but also inventors, etc.). Thus adornments, especially in the form of the trophy, became an expression of power exerted by certain persons; the insignia of power may vary according to the occasions on which they were acquired. Contact with other civilizations had the same effect: the coloured glass beads numerous primitive peoples obtained from the White Man come to mind. The Red Indians in the South Western United States borrowed innumerable pieces of jewellery and ornaments from the earliest Spanish settlers of the sixteenth and seventeenth centuries and developed them in their own way. But it remained significant that immediately after a sudden change in behaviour usually a permanent form established itself and persisted for a long time. This is why we prefer to speak of folk costumes rather than of fashions in the accepted sense. As we shall see, this attitude persisted for a very long time in the development of civilization.

In this context a phenomenon deserves to be mentioned which we find very difficult to explain: this is the sudden standstill of fashion, which for the moment we are interpreting as the transition of fashion to folk costume. Among the North American Indians, for instance, the women of the Navajo and Apache in Arizona and New Mexico adopted the colourful velvet blouses from the Spaniards and have retained them ever since; the same applies to the long, wide skirts taken over from the Anglo-Saxons at the beginning of this century. (This does not mean that there are no changeable fashions, passed on, for instance, from one tribe to another.) We find a similar persistence in the case of the monk's habit; originally, this, too, changed with the fashion. Many parts of the classical clerical vestments are 'fossilized' fashions, such as the cape with hood (the paenula of the ancient Etruscans); the toga of the Roman lawyers became the casula and finally the chasuble of the priest, but also the judge's, advocate's, scholar's, professor's gown, the tunica became the clerical alb; all remained unchanged for centuries, some up to the present time.

The Spanish bullfighters originally changed their dress regularly with the fashion, but suddenly stopped at the end of the eighteenth century so that their costume has remained the same ever since – as can be seen at once in Goya's Tauromachias. As in all the other instances, there seemed to be no specific reason for the sudden freezing of the fashion. Most folk costumes in the narrow sense, however, do not grow among the people, but are 'granted' to them by their rulers, usually on special occasions such as royal engagements and weddings, births, comings of age, accessions to the throne, etc. Clinging to the folk costume here became a symbol of loyalty to a certain ruler or form of rule. It is also interesting to observe that the folk costume was by no means granted as a whole, but in several parts, such as skirt, blouse, cap, belt, buckle, ornaments, as well as colours, materials, and accessories. Usually this development is well documented. This fact alone could make us a little suspicious of claims that the old folk costumes were designed as a whole when most of them can be compared with a patchwork mosaic. But the abrupt paralysis of a fashion that was previously subject to change remains unexplained.

This must not, however, lead us into thinking that primitive man knew only folk costumes, and no fashion at all. The observation of contemporary primitive tribes provide us with various clues that can prevent us from underestimating the appeal of fashion to primitive people. Especially among the so-called half-civilized peoples of India, Southeast Asia, the Far East, Central and South America we find an unusually rapid change of the fashions. The European observer who, with innumerable ideological prejudices, approaches these tribes 'unspoiled by fashion', is all too easily inclined to regard what he sees today as a traditional folk costume, although it may date back only a few years and therefore quite definitely be a fashion. This often applies even to very primitive tribes. Such observers make the mistake of approaching their subjects with preconceived ideas; observations over longer periods of time would perhaps reveal a quite unexpected mobility of the outward behaviour of such tribes. The dominance of the decorative function of dress over any protective function is also very significant in this context. Thus primitive peoples when adopting the White Man's dress often do not wear it as the missionaries expect – as a means of modest concealment – but for precisely the opposite purpose of adornment. To do this they reduce the protective function of dress, which dominates our thinking, to their original decorative desires and adapt it to this end.

How strongly even primitive peoples can succumb to the lure of fashion has been shown by John Adair in his deservedly famous book on the Navajo Indian silversmiths in the South West of the United States. The craft had come to the Navajos about 1875; by about 1895 there were already several hundred silversmiths in the reservation; with incredible speed the new kind of jewellery became a fashion, which just as rapidly spread to the white tourists. Today the production of silver trinkets is enormous, and white and Indian traders outside the reservation cater for lucrative markets in New York, Chicago, Los Angeles, and San Francisco. This spread occurred in several waves: the first silver ornaments did not include precious stones; then the turquoises from New Mexico were used, to be followed, in this order, by those from Iran, Southern Arizona, and Nevada; furthermore, the various tribes (besides the Navajos mainly the Zuni and the Hopi) evolved styles of their own. Here we have an example of the astonishing diversification in the fashion of jewellery among a primitive people.

With hunting trophies it is the indirect significance for fashion that is more pronounced; to begin with, objects brought home from the hunt such as claws, hooves, teeth, hair, ears, brushes, feathers, bones, antlers, horns are worn as distinctive ornaments. In addition the animals' pelts and skins are draped round the body. Naturally, at first their function, too, is decorative and distinctive. But they also have the specific property of affording warmth and protection. This is where we must probably seek the origin of human clothing, which from time immemorial had not only the very rational purpose of protecting the wearer from the severity of the weather, but also a completely irrational importance as a means of distinction and adornment.

This irrationality was most markedly enhanced by the fact that the clothes not only adorned and distinguished their wearers; at the same time they both concealed and drew attention to the primary and secondary sexual characteristics as an expression of the ambivalent attitude of fashion to sex. Although clothes increasingly serve the demands of modesty, they nevertheless also excite desire to reach the source of erotic attraction through them. By concealing they create the irresistible urge to reveal. In addition, this stimulus of curiosity continuously strives to alter the system and means of concealment and display, so that their appeal never weakens. For this very reason clothes were later able to become the most important active expression of fashion, as we can see above all in the consistently ambivalent attitude of mankind to dress. We must, however, stress once again that here, too, religious laws first tend to create permanent forms like folk costumes, exactly as with ornaments proper. It would on the other hand be completely wrong to offer an exclusively technical and rational explanation as if these original forms of dress were purely functional means to protect the body against cold and damp. The fact that even in cool climates we find, besides skins and pelts, other forms of ornamental dress which offer no such protection at all, already disproves this; these forms of 'dress' are simply applied to the skin, temporarily as coloured drawings, permanently as tattoos. Only in extreme conditions, in the Arctic for instance, does the protective function of clothing come more into its own, without, however, losing its secondary, ornamental, character. The countless ornaments in which the decorative function becomes specialized, as it were, and focused are evidence of this. The Australian aborigines were perfectly happy with this ornamental 'dress' until quite recently; even in cold weather they went about completely naked, obtaining warmth only from a glowing log they carried in their hands.

The most important argument along this line, however, refers perhaps to the fact that the original form of dress, a waist string (later waist ring), at first covered or protected nothing at all, but was simply loosely supported by the woman's hip. Only later do we find this string used to hold up a kind of small apron in the front and back; the very way in which it is decorated clearly reveals its purpose as an eyecatcher. Decorations strongly accentuating the back often unduly emphasizing the wearer's buttocks achieve the same effect, and here, too, are meant to be an erotic attraction rather than to afford protection. In other civilizations, such as in Samoa, and in Hawaii, flower garlands and the hula hula serve as dress.

This also indicates another fact, that the original purpose of dressing had nothing to do with modesty; for in extreme cases such a dress conceals nothing. Modesty is perhaps a feeling that occurs only at an extremely advanced stage of civilization and is also extraordinarily complex, with many different motives as well as very marked sociomoral guiding principles concurring in it. Precisely because of the irrational function of decoration and adornment of primitive dress the primary and secondary sexual characteristics are by no means concealed; indeed, they are very often specially emphasized and ostentatiously displayed. Whereas with primitive man this frequently occurred on a massive scale, for instance through a monstrous enlargement of the genitals produced by clothing – especially on the male, more rarely the female (Hottentot apron) – as civilization advanced this assumed progressively more indirect, sublimated, and symbolic forms as modern psychology has been able to demonstrate. Because the taboos modesty imposes have become more and more powerful, the overt decoration and representation of the male and female sex organs becomes less and less prominent; but this development is accompanied by a host of symbolic representations of sex characteristics, for instance in the form of rings and pointed features. Thus the strong indignation at the excessive lengthening of the pointed shoes, often with points specially attached, aroused at the end of the Middle Ages can quite clearly be traced to the generally known sexual symbolism of these shoes. Sometimes the representation was not even symbolic, but quite realistic, in that a phallus was attached to the shoe. Whereas these representations originally left little to the imagination, as for instance in those knightly jousts in honour of the ladies when rings had to be picked up with a lance in the arena, the symbolism became more and more sublimated and refined with increasing sensitivity concerning sexual representations. We shall return to this point presently.

The erotic root survives even in the most cultivated symbolism, even if only in a 'displaced' and subconscious form, and it therefore causes even in our age a quite ambivalent behaviour of the public towards fashion. Modesty is its first and foremost manifestation; it does not as we have already observed appear to be an original behaviour of man. At least its first expressions were already strongly conditioned by conventions and determined by a number of very complex ideas. Evidence of this is the fact that in the course of development of our civilization the sanctions against almost all crimes have become gradually weaker, with the sole exception of those regarding offences against public decency, which have been extraordinarily strengthened. Thus all forms of indecent exposure are punishable today or their perpetrators are forced to undergo psychiatric treatment; primitive man, on the other hand, regarded such actions with more or less indifference.

When we consider the basic features of human dress, in which the purely functional use is at least balanced by all possible irrational impulses (ornaments, distinctions, etc.), we can appreciate that this offered a very promising start to fashion-oriented behaviour (not that this was confined to dress alone). But even if this starting point is established it would be wrong to assume that fashion was effective from the earliest days in the diffused sense that we understand today. Without doubt it was the folk costume that prevailed among the vast majority of early mankind; fashion as a periodical change of style, on the other hand, requires for its effect further impulses, which in our description have so far hardly been mentioned. We nevertheless had to point to the need for decoration and distinction here, because without doubt they represent, among many other elements, roots of fashion which, however, grow fully only with the support of other impulses.

10   Recognition

This will, incidentally, become clear as soon as we trace other functions of decoration and distinction. The decisive difference between these manifestations and fashion change consists in that, although they occur spontaneously and thereby create a change in existing behaviour, they produce definite enduring forms which can be extremely long-lived. One of these manifestations, for instance, is the very simple fact that even the most primitive groups have a tendency of developing a fairly uniform outward general appearance. The outward behaviour then corresponds to the feeling of spiritual affinity. Members of a group thus recognize one another by their costume, their whole manner of deportment, posture and gestures, quite apart from their common language, traditions, ideas, and values, articles of faith, and institutions. This includes all possible techniques which directly affect the body, such as fashions of hairstyle and beard, tattooing, the scarring of forehead, cheek, chest, and other parts, circumcision, the knocking out, pointing, and staining of teeth, perforation of the nostrils and the nasal septum, of cheeks, earlobes, and lips, as well as the wearing of trinkets in the perforation holes – even today people of the Swiss canton of Appenzell still like to wear a gold button in the ear – and finally the alteration of the whole body: smoe South American Indians compress their heads, Chinese women had their feet bandaged until comparatively recently, some tribes induced a special development of the buttocks and the constriction of the waist, which survived into the twentieth century. Something similar often takes place when adolescents become adults; these practices signify membership of the group of the fully-fledged citizens in the community.

The recognition function of dress, ornaments, and general behaviour must, however, be carefully separated from their proper function as a fashion. It is true that in reality both functions usually merge: for instance, part of the effect of a new song hit is based on the fact that we feel pleasurable satisfaction when we recognize it; but because all processes in the socio-human civilization are extraordinarily complex, even a frequent (if not regular) common occurrence of certain traits must not mislead us into simply lumping them materially together. Naturally the heightened influence of fashion on certain sections of society has the secondary effect that members of these sections recognize one another by this trait. But here the function of recognition has quite different consequences to fashion-oriented behaviour. Recognition is possible only provided certain permanent traits exist. Here the constant trait would be that certain classes of society regularly display a certain wealth (and can afford to do so), a display which is either deliberately rejected by other groups and classes or at least, mainly for economic reasons, not practised. Here, then, the rapid change in fashion becomes a sign of recognition; one feels one owes it to one's social position to follow every minute change, and on the strength of this regards oneself as 'belonging'. But the whole behaviour is related in a purely formal manner to the accelerated rhythm of fashion change, not yet to its individual contents. We thus must, in spite of the occasional closest approximation of the two phenomena, keep a strict distinction between them.

We can see this most readily if we follow the various effects of this recognition function of dress. We have already become familiar with one case: members of one and the same group are

12. Madame Récamier (by David), the Queen of the Directorate. An anticipation of the see-through look. The breasts are supported by the high waist
Staatsbibliothek Berlin

13. *(Far left)* High Society: Mr and Mrs Hobson at the races, Paris (1914). *Modebuch Verlagsgesellschaft, Zürich*

14. *(Left)* A hippie couple, Isle of Man Pop Festival (1970). *dpa*

able to recognize one another by their fairly similar outward appearance. The extreme case is the uniform and uniform behaviour, which in certain groups is called upon to play an important role, for example, among the military; members of certain orders, associations, societies and so on, too, use extremely similar dress. But we have already noted earlier that radical uniformity is extremely rare; thus the similarity of dress generally does not go very far. It is usually enough if the general lines are followed, within which the individual is allowed a certain latitude, without damage to the recognition function. An example of this, at least in part, is the difference between male and female dress. Since it can be shown that in human society this anthropologically basic difference has played an extraordinary role from the very beginning, we must not be surprised that all the religious ideas associated with the distinction between the sexes must express themselves in the dress. This produces certain permanent types, which are regularly controlled by customs (and thereby religious sanctions when we allow for the distinctly religious magic character of the original sexual taboos). Conversely the exchange of clothing, especially when men wear women's clothes, but also vice versa, is regarded as a grave sin, although it occurs again and again, even in an institutionally controlled way as among a number of North American Indian tribes on the Great Plains. Even the hero Achilles is said to have been sent to King Lycomedes by his father Peleus, to save him from death in battle, and that he lived there disguised as a girl with the King's daughters until Ulysses discovered him by means of a ruse.

What applies to the distinction between the sexes also applies to the various ages; we find clearly differentiated forms of dress among the various age groups. What a given society thinks of its children can be most clearly seen in its children's clothing. Where the child is regarded as a 'little adult', dress is the same for everyone; here only the distinction between the sexes is observed. Where, however, the life-style of the child is considered to be something apart, the children have their own style of dress. The same applies to the adolescents, young girls and boys; here we must stress a striking difference in the present age: whereas we take it completely for granted today that young girls should have fashions of their own, basically different from those of older women, dress for young boys and grown men is extraordinarily alike. We shall see later that this expresses a basic trait of male fashion, which has its own historical roots and is evidence of a male attitude to fashion that considerably differs from the female. We shall also discuss the fact that one can see from the varying degrees of distinction between male and female dress how greatly a certain civilization or period of style rates the difference between the sexes.

A number of differentiations that also create their own dress must be added to the differences between the sexes and the age groups; above all the special dress of professions and trades and certain persons of authority (priests, chieftains, magicians, princes) or of groups of persons of authority, such as aristocrats, who usually proclaimed their rank by assuming certain privileges of cut or colour of their dress or of their outward appearance (e.g. long hair, particularly elaborate tattoos, feathers of certain birds, special colours such as the red piping of the toga of Roman senators, or the various hues of red and purple of the various ranks of the clergy etc.), privileges which the rest of the population did not share. Ultimately the development of the social ladder was carried to the stage where every class and within each class individual subgroups wore their own dress. This class-based dress carried the recognition function to its extreme, externally as well as internally, so that in this type of society it became possible to identify the class of every single person simply by the dress he wore. Pictorial representations of this kind are numerous, such as the famous illuminated manuscript of the Sachsenspiegel (Mirror of the Saxons).

The question of dress as an indicator of social rank is in several respects of the utmost importance for the understanding of fashion, and so we must briefly discuss it. For there is an old theory of fashion (also formulated by Herbert Spencer) according to which the fashion movement is created by the imitation of the upper by the lower classes; the upper classes are thereby forced – in order to maintain their distinction from the masses – to change their fashion, until the others catch up with them again, when the cycle starts again. Although this idea survives directly or indirectly in many passages of the relevant literature, it must be considered untenable today for several reasons. What we can safely accept of it is the notion of dress as a means of distinction. But this led, first via the crystallization of these marks of distinction in customs, to the already repeatedly mentioned permanent forms, which were not imitated because it was forbidden to do so; this would, after all, have constituted a breach of the customs, which were mostly sanctioned by the Church. Conversely this makes the outrage understandable which often showed in the so-called 'dress regulations' castigating the lower estates for wanting to imitate their social superiors. Such a behaviour was branded as offensive not in the sense that the imitators were morally offensive, but because of their disregard of the existing traditional forms of life. The strict class order of society thus knew only differentiation, but no imitation; at the earliest imitation occurred only when the existing social order began to disintegrate. We therefore cannot claim that the principal origin of fashion should be traced to the class structure in that the lower estates imitated the upper ones, thus forcing them to change their style of dress continuously. Imitation started only when the class order began to break up.

We must now consider a completely different question: whether there are fashion impulses within the upper ranks of the social order that make the higher-placed and the rich compete with one another in the fashion game. Quite obviously fashion rivalry exists within the upper estates but not between them unless the old order is in a state of complete disintegration.

Thus the already quoted S. R. Steinmetz reaches the following conclusion:

> In the typical corporate state fashion manifests itself very little; the highest class is an exception, but there is not a trace of class rivalry; only if this order shows cracks, fashion will become evident; when the alleged basis disappears, fashion reaches its full flower. Class and fashion therefore do not wax and wane in parallel; where one is strong, the other is absent and vice versa. The final conclusion ... is incontrovertible that the estates structure is not the root cause of fashion, and that Spencer's generally accepted theory of fashion is wrong.

We can continue this argument by claiming that it is not the estates system but a more general phenomenon which largely decides the progress of fashion: the rivalry between the leaders of the upper classes. To appreciate the full significance of this we have only to realize that in the old estates system an enormous number of people were required to maintain a quite minute upper class and to enable its members to live lives of leisure; whereas the lower classes remained apathetic, the leaders of this system unfolded not only political, organizational, and cultural activities, but also created fashions, from which they strove to exclude everybody else. Sometimes they were highly successful in this.

11 Rivalry and Competition

In spite of these very negative preliminary results, we have found a starting point to direct us farther. Although it is without doubt correct that in a strict estates system no fashion influence exists between the various estates, it is also certain that strong fashion changes occur within the upper estates. Any history of costumes illustrates this sufficiently. We can generally say that in any clearly stratified society, in which not only individuals in positions of authority, but entire groups, which may be estates or aristocracies, dominated other subordinate groups, a distinct rivalry existed in every respect within the upper group or groups. Where only a single family, say the chieftain's, enjoyed special privileges, such a movement was hardly found. As soon as there were several privileged families, a regular situation at the beginning of feudalism, strong rivalry immediately arose, and this acquired the greatest importance for the development of fashion.

We find even in the most primitive civilizations many expressions of rivalry and competition, for instance when different tribes meet and establish a mutual connection. Hardly ever (or only after a very long time) will the result of such a meeting be straightforward fusion; on the contrary, in spite of all connections considerable tensions in the fight for hegemony usually occur, which can express themselves in the most varied ways. An important occasion on which such tensions become evident is the exchange of women between the two tribes and the subsequent marriage ceremonies; here rivalry usually manifests itself prominently in competitive ostentation and exchange of presents. Of particular interest to us in this context is an institution in primitive civilizations whose full significance has been realized only recently. This is the so-called potlatch institution of the Indians of the American Northwest, the Tlinkit, Haida, and Kwakiutl, which plays a most important role in distinction. We are inclined today to see in it one of the roots of feudalism. The word 'potlatch' means 'to nourish', or 'to consume'; we have, firstly, a manifestation of the sphere of consumption, in which, after all, fashion, too, has its place. Potlatch, by outward appearances, is a feast with a bias towards rivalry, in which the host by the very act of his invitation vaguely challenges his guest or guests in whose honour the feast has been arranged. The organization of the feast (it is obligatory if the host does not want to lose his social standing) as well as the acceptance of the invitation are regulated by ceremony. The acceptance includes the duty to reciprocate. In practice this creates a competition without end if the participants want to maintain their social positions. Some time ago the great Dutch cultural historian Jan Huizinga stressed the playful element of this institution; indeed there is the closest possible connection between this very long-established custom, the agonistics of the ancient Greeks, and the tournaments of the European knights in the Middle Ages.

The potlatch ceremony is very complex. Its character is at the same time ritual, economic, social, and legal. It is economic in that economic products are exchanged in an ostentatious manner; it is social in that the products are exchanged simply to gain social rank, title, and a coat of arms; it is legal in that it entails certain obligations to give products in return for those received (usually at quite usurious interest); it is ritual in that it represents only the sector of a comprehensive ritual cycle in which this system of presents and return presents is accommodated. This institution, which is of the utmost importance for the development of power in human society, also shows an enhancement and a radicalization of the already mentioned primeval need for distinction which so brightly illuminates our problem of fashion. We must also add that the potlatch ceremony is not unique but that such institutions have been found in a large number of primitive societies and in the advanced ancient civilizations.

The rivalry between the representatives of the wealthy extends to open conflict, the individual duel, or war, and in certain circumstances ends even with the killing of the chieftains and noblemen meeting one another in the competition. In this game one group of relatives regularly faces another such group; both stake all their worldly goods; the real protagonists are the heads of the families; the rest makes up the spectators. The games are accompanied by an often amazing ostentation before the eyes of the public. This provokes the adversary into trying to outbid the challenger and spurs him to higher and higher achievement. He who is able to spend most in this pomp and display is the final victor. If he wants to draw special attention to his victory, he will climb a precipice above the sea and throw a lot of valuables into the water. The demonstrative splendour of wealth and waste is consummated with a demonstrative destruction of riches. But that the contest also concerns social rank is proved by the very fact that the most valuable indicators of wealth are copper plates with family crests engraved on them. Eventually the victor takes over the titles, coat of arms, possessions, women, members of the family, slaves, land, and all the other privileges of the loser. On the other hand he cannot refuse if the latter asks for a return 'fixture'.

Thus there is indeed a feud without end, with a striking, playful element in it. After the first discovery of this institution among the Indians of the American Northwest, a whole range of related intermediate forms from the simplest distinctions to these quite agonistic ceremonies were found among a large number of other primitive tribes, for example, in Oceania (Polynesians and Melanesians), the advanced ancient civilizations and the Middle Ages in Europe. Thus events at which two or more contestants compete with one another with presents and amiable speeches are extremely widespread; elaborate forms of address and rivalry in titles and other, visible, forms of distinction (such as medals and similar decorations) likewise belong to this category. As a curiosity we find duels of abuse among the Homeric Greeks, present-day Eskimos, and many other peoples. Lastly we play the same game in our everyday social life, during celebrations, weddings, parties, where we are obliged by etiquette to return the hospitality received, that is 'to revenge ourselves' for it. The term 'revenge' clearly indicates the original combative character of this behaviour.

The controlled nature of such manifestations is seen in the strangest light when we look at the giving of presents. In our average awareness we believe that we can see in the giving of presents an act of purest spontaneity and warm-hearted purpose. A glance at the development of the giving of presents in human society, however, shows that even this is governed by a rigid social code regarding both the occasions and the kind of giving, as the French sociologist Marcel Mauss was the first to discover. Here a threefold obligation appears, firstly that of giving presents on certain occasions, secondly that of accepting them, and thirdly that of giving presents in return after an also regulated period of time. Those who do not observe the third obligation 'lose face' as the Chinese say, in other words here, too, the motive of loss of status is still involved although in a less radical form than with the potlatch. Here is another example: in Samoa, tribal chiefs exchange ornamental mats during weddings; not only during weddings, but really on any suitable occasion: births, circumcisions, illnesses, initiation rites for boys and girls, funeral ceremonies, as well as trade expeditions. This custom expresses two concepts: firstly the principle of honour, prestige, 'mana', a kind of mysterious force which creates, among other things, wealth; and secondly the absolute obligation of reciprocating with other presents at the risk of losing 'mana' and with it the authority and wealth derived from its possession when the person obliged fails to do so. After the ceremony the participants are seen, from a direct and rational angle, to be no richer but actually poorer than before. They feel, however, the satisfaction of having displayed and given away a lot of wealth on some occasion or other. This safeguards and possibly enhances their rank, thus indirectly offering them the chance of acquiring new wealth. No matter how irrational such actions may appear in the light of modern economic considerations, they really represent, from the last-mentioned point of view, an 'investment', which is perhaps not intentional, but occurs as an 'ancillary consequence' of the behaviour described.

The development of the potlatch ceremony among the Kwakiutl on Vancouver Island, where it was investigated in great detail up to quite recently (by Helen Codere, for example, in 1950) shows some further peculiarities, which one must be familiar with to be able fully to assess the significance of this institution. Firstly, potlatch quite clearly does not fit in the framework of a pure subsistence economy; because consumption is not based merely on need, but far exceeds it. Nor does it fit in the framework of the so-called market economy, although the Kwakiutl especially produce very efficiently for the world market (mainly tinned salmon). On the contrary, the whole complex belongs to a particular economic system which has been called 'prestige economy', because here rivalry is mainly about status and honour. Added to this is the fact that they amassed their wealth completely without effort, because in those latitudes the salmon literally swam into the hands of the fisher before industrially organized fishing reduced their numbers more and more. This wealth, combined with the special climatic conditions, which during the long arctic night make work impossible, creates an annually recurring period of general leisure; this forms the background of these competitions. Thus a uniform situation is established in which effortless wealth, leisure, and agonistics combine and in a kind of 'dionysiac ecstasis' as Ruth Benedict calls it, magnify the technique of this peculiar 'property contest' to an extreme degree. This superiority of the contestants over their rivals is celebrated in innumerable songs, with all the participants active in a single huge festive event, which we have already seen to be a very important factor in the spread of fashion during and after the Middle Ages.

> I am the great chief who shames everybody
> I am the great chief who shames everybody
> Our chief makes everybody blush with shame
> Our chief makes everybody jealous
> Our chief makes people hide their faces,
> From all he does again and again in the world,
> Because he always arranges new oil-feasts
> for all the tribes.

In spite of all attempts by the White Man and the missionaries to wean the Kwakiutl from their ancient custom, not only has this institution persisted to our days, but the volume of the goods transacted during the competition has steadily increased.

Phenomena of this kind, to which innumerable others could be added, show the far-reaching roots of fashion in various basic human-social behaviour patterns, and also the mainspring of fashion among the upper estates. This is without doubt competition in all its various forms. From this angle we can build up a special conception for describing these competing kinds of exchange goods, which is also of great importance for fashion. This is the conception of 'conspicuous consumption' introduced by the U.S. economist Thorstein Veblen, which is also most closely connected with the previously mentioned prestige economy. The preconditions for this style of life are leisure and abstention from economic activity, as the title of one of his main works (*Theory of the Leisure Class*) indicates. We have already encountered this situation in the potlatch institution. It is of special importance in that here the phenomenon of 'luxury' and of luxury consumption, which has a very important association with the development of fashion among the upper classes, makes its debut. But it is even more important that consumption has no longer the purpose of merely satisfying tangible needs, but both of aggressively demonstrating the consumer's own social position to the public and if possible even of enhancing it during competition with rivals in the form of a challenge. We realize the connection between the feudal-class development of power and a special style of consumption whose characteristics we are now about to outline.

This style of consumption involves not only spending on items beyond the actual necessities of life: at the same time the objects of consumption become specialized. From this stage onwards they increase not only in numbers, they are also qualitatively modified in the sense of becoming 'refined'. Although this could be understood as a measure of making consumer goods more suitable for direct consumption through special treatment and preparation, the underlying purpose is different: their modification serves the 'canon of reputability' – decency and respectability – on which in the last resort the prestige of the upper classes rests. It is therefore not only essential that the goods consumed should be better than others, but even more so that they are consumed in a certain, conventionally controlled way which precludes any form of random consumption. Here begins the entire scale of conventional forms of consumption, which very often started as quite demonstrative forms and distinct fashions among the upper classes; later they may have developed permanent forms (such as eating with knife and fork) which gradually spread throughout the whole of society. We shall presently return to this point.

This style of consumption must, with the increase of wealth and of economic goods in human society, become more and more sharply outlined; we can find its purest form in the system of feudalism. The persistence with which this particular order of society asserted itself is connected with, among other reasons, the fact that it historically expressed basic human as well as social behaviour patterns. This development became even more accentuated as the class system developed further and further and became more complicated (for example, during the age of absolutism). For then the simple distinction from the lower classes was immediately augmented by the internal rivalry between the various upper classes (such as the temporal and clerical aristocracies) and between the individual members of the various upper classes. This, however, also meant rivalry in presents, festivities and ceremonies of all kinds, which we have already mentioned, and above all rivalry in fashion.

Thorstein Veblen mentioned the potlatch ceremony in this context, although the real discussion of the significance of this institution began considerably later. He was also aware of other roots of such and similar institutions, for example, the banqueting societies (commensuality) in the service both of religious edification and the confirmation of certain communal bonds, which in everyday life are easily weakened and loosened. It became evident especially in the feudal system that demonstrative consumption was by no means restricted to the leaders of society, but also spread to the followers who in ostentative and ceremonial consumption did honour not only to themselves, but also to their masters. Competition between the great noblemen naturally spread to their retinue even if it was tacitly admitted that its behaviour was not 'original', but 'imitative', vicarious, as it were. This is where the problem of imitation acquired its peculiar significance for the theory of fashion, as we shall soon demonstrate. In the course of the spread of ceremonial consumption from the lords and masters to their liegemen there was constant stress on solidarity (it was thus by no means a fashion competition between the classes, but exclusively between the various groups of the upper class). This happened regularly on a large number of different occasions, such as the previously mentioned great communal festivities, during which the various groups demonstratively confirmed their solidarity to themselves as well as to the other groups. This was sometimes used even as a political lever, for instance, by Louis XIV, who systematically attracted the great nobility to his court at Versailles to promote 'absenteeism' – the absence of the aristocratic families from their estates – and to break the independence of the feudal masters in the provinces. Their functions could then increasingly be taken over by ennobled officials (*noblesse de robe*) and the bourgeoisie, both under obligation to the absolute monarchy. During those festivities, at which the entire upper classes congregated, the originally religious and community-strengthening function of this institution occasionally became very tangibly evident, even if it was aesthetically diluted, as it were. The commensuality of the king and his aristocratic followers created and over and over again strengthened a kind of mystical unity. Although the aristocrats were ruined at the end of the festivities, they returned home in heightened splendour. But history decreed that this return became a full retreat: the new forces of the bourgeoisie had meanwhile occupied one economic position after another.

We note a similar development in Japan during the eighteenth century, where the Tokugawa regime concentrated the competing aristocrats in the capital (then called Edo) to keep them under more effective political control. This created not only an enormous market for luxury products, but also a huge concentration of the population. The metropolis already had more than a million and a half inhabitants when London and Paris were still below one million; at the same time the city became a genuine centre of fashion. Similar political constellations thus create similar developments in fashion.

12 Conspicuousness and Approval

In the preceding chapter we traced an important source of fashion, which runs from the simplest forms of distinction to real competition. This competition between the upper strata of a society regularly resulted in a first intensive development of fashion among the representatives of leading groups in the various aristocracies and class systems from antiquity to the end of the Middle Ages and even to the height of royal absolutism. As long as these systems were stable and intrinsically secure, the lower classes knew only a slight fashion movement as a periodical change in style; they clung mainly to their folk costumes, which they were sometimes openly 'granted' by their feudal lords, mostly on festive occasions such as weddings, christenings, etc. The system was disturbed only where, for instance, the urban patricians began to manoeuvre into positions of equality with the old feudal nobility. This moment in turn heralded the onset of competition between the patricians and the feudal nobles as well as between the different ranks of the patricians. In both cases the winners always tried to keep the losers at bay with dress regulations and bans on luxuries (sumptuary laws). A basic change in the situation occurred only after the class systems had been undermined by social, political, and economic developments.

By ascribing this important role in fashion to competition we naturally do not imply that its effect is confined solely to fashion. On the contrary, exactly like curiosity it has many other and much more important functions, such as in the development of political power and institutional rule. But the fact that fashion draws on a fundamental force which is of such immense importance in the development of civilization shows us once again how wrong we are in underestimating its significance. But before we follow fashion to its true climax, we must first trace its more elementary laws of movement, which so far have been in evidence only partly and indirectly.

'Conspicuousness' is without doubt the prime mover of the already described processes. The striving for distinction seems to be an innate characteristic of man. It is expressed in the effort not only to accomplish outstanding deeds in some field or other, but equally to produce tangible evidence of these achievements and parade them. We find this, as we have previously shown, already among primitive peoples, where distinction serves to emphasize both a personal performance and distinctive features of certain constituent groups (men and women, age groups, professions and trades, ranks, etc.). The main initial function of distinction is therefore differentiation or discrimination. It thus happens that at first sight a certain aloofness of varying degrees begins to separate those distinguished (as groups or as individuals) from the rest. The Frenchman Edmond Goblot went so far as to call it a 'barrier', which at first was insurmountable (this is why very strict limits were imposed on direct imitation).

We must now deal with another question, very closely connected with what we have just discussed and introducing very important further elements of fashion. This question is very simple: What use is the most beautiful distinction if it is not recognized by the public? Thus the distinction, if it is to function effectively by making conspicuous, distinguishing its wearer, must be associated with something that is accepted by the community as a distinctive feature. Every distinction must therefore also be part and parcel of the entire complex of traditional values handed down by our forebears, and accepted by the rest of the community. This instantly leads to another paradox: distinction from and forming part of a social group do not rule each other out. A person can distinguish himself only in so far as he does something that is acknowledged by the community. He thus bows to the judgement of the community at precisely the moment when he seeks to excel the members of the community. This expresses a curious sociological principle: even distinction and differentiation from the rest of the community need not infringe the system of social integration, i.e. the acceptance of judgements, valuations, and opinions of the community (the cases in which this happens we shall soon recognize as true limiting cases). This would again suggest a certain measure of caution regarding the concept of 'reaching a state of uniformity'. This state would be the extreme expression of social integration; but if in reality this does not preclude distinction and differentiation, it also means that this drift towards uniformity in the sociological sense need by no means be identical with sameness or conformism. The immediate consequences of this realization for the understanding of fashion are tangible. With its inescapable alternation between change and stability fashion certainly approaches uniformity. But it still leaves room for purely personal deviations from the general line; these, however, are also subject to social regulation, which means that they are limited. The rigid lines of etiquette are softened by personal tact and taste. Distinction and integration are therefore not contradictory, since integration does not imply an obligation to conform.

Distinction is based on 1) an action or behaviour thought by the community to be important and distinctive or really useful and valuable to it; 2) the acceptance by the community of the symbol of distinction, and 3) a ceremonial behaviour thought to be appropriate to the distinction, i.e. the canon of reputability we have already mentioned. Distinction and integration go hand in hand in all three points. There can be no distinction outside the framework of social recognition; it would be inherently pointless. The third point, the required ceremonial behaviour, reveals this most clearly. Here the already quoted Goblot has connected the concept of 'barrier' with that of 'standard', which has to be maintained if the barrier – the distinction – is to prove its effectiveness.

The decisive function connecting these two elements expresses itself in a kind of formalization of behaviour, also called 'ritualization'. This adds nothing material to the means employed to establish distinction; the tea used in the Japanese tea ceremony is not improved by the ceremony as such. In fact, the ritualization always refers only to the accompanying circumstances, which it forces into a fixed, predetermined sequence. It often develops into special phrases and manners of speaking. All religions from the very beginning have profoundly appreciated the 'uplifting' function of such ritualized sequences, as the role of the 'rite' in any religious ceremony proves. In the rite, the freely developing spontaneity of religious emotions is cast in a firm mould, which can be reproduced and therefore communicated from person to person. The rite has thus acquired an enormous power to draw the community together.

This very ritualization, however, also constitutes its limit, because 'ritualization' can end in completely unthinking performance. The 'standard', which, as it were, has become subconscious, can then no longer act as a 'barrier'; it will appear merely as an empty gesture, an expressionless rigmarole, whose sole effect is that of an escape from spontaneity, and therefore, naturally, also from creativeness. Clearly the ritualization of the striving for distinction is a particularly obvious development because the real positions of power which usually accompany a distinction no longer exist. Thus ritualization of distinction behaviour is a typical behaviour pattern of individuals, groups, or social strata that are long past their prime. After the 'old days of glory' have gone, all that remains as justification is the elaborate ritualism for its own sake, like the prayer mill after the force of religious fervour has spent itself. On the other hand, this tendency towards ritualization continues to receive, even after the concrete circumstances sustaining it have ceased to exist, support from a general biological bias in favour of the ritual.

13 Imitation

We have already seen that distinction bears within itself a possibility of undisguised evolution into rivalry, prominent mainly among the dominant groups of stratified societies. The outstanding and appreciated feat gives rise to envy, secret ambition, and efforts to equal those in more highly esteemed positions. It is essential to human social life that individuals and groups strive for distinction; it is equally characteristic of social man that the many always seek to match the few who have distinguished themselves in one way or another; in fact they endeavour to excel them if they can. This is indeed the meaning of rivalry and of agonistics.

To explain this development a certain theory was often quoted in the past, which has become so well known that it merits discussion in some detail. It is the theory of 'imitation', used to explain how the losers in a competition become more like the winners. The Frenchman Gabriel Tarde, incidentally one of the most brilliant fashion analysts, sees imitation even as the basic principle of social life. Herbert Spencer, too, accords this concept considerable importance, as we have already indicated; he thinks that the lower classes by their imitation compel the upper classes to change their fashion so that they can preserve their distinction from their social inferiors. It was the German philosopher Georg Simmel, however, who offered the most closely reasoned argument in favour of imitation as the basis of fashion. Developing Tarde's and Spencer's ideas further, he clearly summarized his opinion as follows:

> Imitation . . . offers the individual the reassurance that he is not alone in his actions; it rises above the past practice of the same activity as on a firm base, which relieves present practice of the difficulty of supporting itself . . . Whenever we imitate, we devolve not only the need for productive energy, but also the responsibility for these activities from ourselves upon others; this frees the individual from the necessity of making a choice and simply accords him the role of a member of a group, of a vessel of social contents . . . The conditions in which fashion exists as an enduring manifestation in the history of our species are thus outlined. It is the imitation of a given pattern and therefore satisfies the need for social support, it leads the individual on to the track everybody else follows, it offers a general norm which reduces the behaviour of every individual to a mere pattern.'

In the last resort Simmel regards imitation on this basis as something 'sired by thought out of thoughtlessness'.

The basic idea of this thesis postulates that imitation, starting from an initial triggering action, creates mighty currents which cause uniform action among the masses. The importance of this thesis increases because imitation is a principle which seems to reach far beyond the confines of human society, playing as it does an extraordinary part in the animal kingdom. But this very fact raises important questions, which we have to study at least briefly to illustrate our problems further. Think of the example of a hen and its chickens. The hen pecks, and the chickens imitate their mother. Is what they do really imitation, 'learning through imitation', or is it something entirely different? In fact it is the latter. All the mother bird's pecking, its scratching and calling does is trigger a disposition already present in the chicken. What superficially appears to be imitation is in reality nothing of the kind. Here (as in the already mentioned flight of a herd of wild animals during danger) the uniformity of the action is established by the effect of a certain external stimulus which triggers the same instinctive reactions among all the animals affected. Even in the animal the problem of imitation is therefore by no means as simply based as it would appear at first sight.

With social man the situation is more difficult and complex, to begin with because in man we must allow not only for instincts and driving forces but also for his social organization. What is more, we find a whole scale of intermediate forms between these extremes. We must above all bear in mind that man may occasionally imitate quite consciously, like the Japanese, who have imitated the West's system of industrial production since 1868. They did this solely because of purely rational considerations of planning their future. But since we have repeatedly pointed out the irrational elements of fashion, we must in this context disregard this type of imitation, which is at the extreme end of the scale. The simplest self-examination shows us generally that imitation hardly ever occurs spontaneously, automatically as it were. But there are some factors which promote and some which inhibit it. It undoubtedly promotes imitation if we are in some way connected with the subject of our imitation. Prominent factors can be: sympathy, admiration, or respect for the wisdom, the position etc. of the person we imitate. But it is always necessary for a certain relationship to exist between the imitator and the imitated. From this fact we derive the principle that imitation is by no means random; it occurs exclusively along already existing social connections; the person imitated can be either an equal or a superior. This also implies that imitation does not by itself create social relationship, it is merely one of several symptoms of already existing relationships and one of its most important functions is the more intensive development of them. This principle is confirmed when we look at the other side of the problem, the inhibition of imitation. When do we feel the most intense aversion from imitating some other person? Surely whenever this person's way of acting and thinking appears strange or senseless to us. The person may be mad in the strictest sense of the term, which altogether excludes our readiness for imitation; this refusal to imitate because of excessively irrational behaviour is the opposite of purely rationally motivated imitation. But the other person may merely belong to a strange civilization with a different style of life; the experience of strangeness will inhibit us from imitating a certain action no matter how sensible it may be. We must point out in this context how easily the masses are inclined to consider people 'mad' who react in a different way because they belong to a different civilization.

Such an inhibition of imitation is found not only between different civilizations, but (as we have already seen) even within one and the same civilization between the representatives of various strata, professions, and classes as long as the system of stratification is still intact. Representatives of the same class – precisely because of their feeling of solidarity – always have a tendency to develop a kind of uniformity of behaviour. Here, then, we have effective imitation. At the same time they attempt to prevent all imitation by social inferiors whom they in turn refuse to imitate (with a few exceptions, to which we shall return later). The safeguarding of the social standard demands the erection of a 'barrier' against the lowlier. This does not by any means prevent the current leader from becoming the subject of imitation within the fabric of the top classes; we have already mentioned the fashion competition inside the upper estates. Conversely, imitation from below was not only expressly prevented (for instance by dress regulations or sumptuary laws), the lower classes usually did not even feel the need for it as long as the class order was still rigid and appeared as a God-given subordination of the lower to the upper classes; there were even often attempts to ascribe different qualities to members of different classes, as for instance in Plato's *Republic*. To this corresponded the often-described paralysing influence the top of the social scale exerted on the bottom in these class systems; the fact that this social order usually seemed sanctioned by religious laws only reinforced the tendency.

Another circumstance important in an explanation of how relatively uniform behaviour can evolve must be mentioned in this connection. Existing social bonds should not be thought of only in terms of innumerable purely individual and human relationships. There are also socio-economic dispositions which are common to a society as a whole or at least to individual constituent groups in it. We then speak of objective 'social situations' which may correspond to a dominant kind of economic activity, a special approach to property, or a relationship of political subjugation. In such cases large masses of people have reacted in a relatively uniform way, although this does not entitle us to speak of imitation in the strict sense of the word. Rather it was a uniform action arising out of identical living conditions from which a special 'life style' grew. Here, naturally, the enduring forms of folk costume and behaviour already discussed fell into place. It is obvious that this must materialize more strongly than anywhere else among the lower groups, which especially in the old class systems were, and most intensely in the caste system of India still are, at the same time associated by fate with their economic occupations in that they were born into their station and unable ever to escape it.

The upper class, on the other hand, was less restricted both in the political and generally social sense and in the field of fashion: to the upper classes leisure was the purest manifestation of the relief from all economic pressures and the relatively uniform behaviour they engender, so that especially here the changeable fashion made its debut beside the folk costume, particularly during rivalry between various upper groups or persons. The trade of war alone, which originally characterized the upper classes, could not change this situation if only because it did not constitute a permanent profession. What we are left with, then, is that imitation as such does not establish any social relations but merely reinforces already existing ones and gives them a meaningful expression.

All this need not surprise us if we bear in mind that every imitation must be preceded by an act of perception and acceptance of something different; otherwise it constitutes no more than simple aping, which may occur purely individually but can never give rise to social currents. And such an acceptance and perception of what is different naturally presupposes certain common features, a cultural continuum as it were, whose limits can mostly be readily outlined. What is wholly extravagant cannot be imitated if only because it is beyond understanding. Although some nevertheless understand it because of some special knowledge they possess, the others, whose acceptance is essential if imitation is to take root, do not.

We must add in conclusion that this field of associations in certain strata of life can occasionally expand enormously. This applies particularly to the present age which, at least in the Western civilizations, is beginning to generate a kind of fairly uniform cultural atmosphere. It can then happen that the Prince of Wales's valet creases his master's trousers, or that the Prince himself forgets to close the last button of his waistcoat, and that first a certain social set in Europe and ultimately in the whole world copies him. This brings us face to face with some quite different problems, this time purely historical in that they express a basic feature peculiar to our present age, which gradually produces a kind of 'international public'. This 'international set' is united only in a narrowly restricted sphere of life. No matter how disunited the nations may be politically, they agree in the admiration of a few personalities (sports, film, etc.).

14 Performers and Spectators

Another basic social relationship whose weight has also recently been recognized is, however, of greater significance than imitation in the development of fashion. When we claim that distinction and acknowledgement cannot be separated from each other, we can illustrate this in a concrete manner by showing the relationship between performers and spectators; the special importance of the eye for fashion consciousness has already been mentioned. Approval is thus a prerequisite of distinction, and distinction sometimes even tries to gain it deliberately. At the very moment when distinction courts approval it inevitably arouses in those that show their approval the desire also to acquire a share in the distinction. The erstwhile spectator offering applause wants to become a performer himself, also to be applauded. The German sociologist Alfred Vierkandt spoke of an 'exchange of roles between performers and spectators' in this context. The profound connection of this relationship and the continually possible change of perspective with the phenomenon of competition is too obvious for any special explanation.

    This exchange of roles thus regularly produces a situation in which those who first applauded the person that has distinguished himself seek to gain the same distinction and accordingly make use of the same relevant symbol of distinction. This illustrates afresh that imitation (if we want to speak of imitation at all in this context) functions only inside a circle of groups within which this interchange between spectators and performers is possible. The constantly recurring alternation between, for instance, performers and spectators gradually leads to the spread of some special symbol of distinction throughout the entire group in question. But since the whole is part and parcel of a continuous competition, no end can be seen in principle to such an interplay.

Apart from the fact that spectators of the competition of fashion always have a stimulating effect on the performers and thus carry rivalry to extremes, their special function is to watch that the rules of the game are observed for the maintenance of the accepted standards. Here again there is the closest possible connection between the spectators on the one side and customs, convention, etiquette and the canon of reputability on the other. The spectators represent, as it were, public opinion in a group which, however, by the very act of judging the others (the performers) commits itself; for the relationship between spectator and performer can at any time be reversed since it is mutual.

This reveals a new basic fact, which is also of the greatest importance for fashion. For in this continual reversal of the relationship between performers and spectators, everybody will very soon have obtained a certain distinction, which means that nobody is distinguished any more. This would suggest a continuous competition-induced self-destruction of fashion, inevitably arising out of the basic social relation of the interplay between performers and spectators. At first fashion is a mark of distinction; but through the medium of approval, without which it cannot exist, though the competition, which immediately follows approval, in the interchange of the roles of spectators and performers and though the ambition to rival the creators of fashion the distinction gradually disappears and becomes commonplace.

The average process runs a regular course and at the end a fashion disappears as suddenly as it appeared. Hence the reputation of levity that fashion has acquired, although the term is not quite correct. For this apparent levity hides a restless, consuming death-wish, which is realized at the precise moment when a fashion has reached its climax and basks in the eager acceptance of the great public. Hence the veil of melancholy that surrounds every fashion. It serves to enhance beauty and enliven the drabness of everyday life; but it is its inescapable destiny to die by its own laws and its own hands at the youthful age of precocious perfection. Naturally, this law which governs the development of fashion has the most far-reaching economic consequences, because the funeral pyre of the many dead fashions consists of what the trade calls 'dead stock'. This is why the fashion trade must always ensure that the remnants of fashion articles are disposed of as quickly as possible before they have time to become real white elephants. This is one of the functions of the biannual sales. Usually the production of particularly fashion-affected articles must be stopped as soon as they have reached the market and the consumers.

After a fashion has run its course, that is, found its own level and at the same time reached its own end, immediately a nagging curiosity, which we have recognized as the general human root of fashion, begins to reassert itself. Thus the fashion game starts afresh in innumerable variations, to which basically no end can be foreseen. The appearance of new features need not mean a total change of style; it is often confined to details, trimmings, accessories. This change of details, however, is continuous although, as the history of fashion confirms, the great breaks in style are relatively rare. But this comes to light only in the sober analysis of the historian; contemporaries usually have no eye for the difference between change of detail and change of style. This is especially true of the snob of every description who is inclined to promote every slightest change to a true change of style.

The fashion snob is a man who believes he owes it to the spectators to follow every single trend, no matter how eccentric, and to display it prominently. His most outstanding trait is the seriousness with which he blows up every variant into a question of life and death and his uncritical acceptance of everything without checking whether the new idea will pass the test of public approval; he must always be ahead of his time – as a matter of principle. One can say that the fashion snob exaggerates the general social function of fashion to such an extent that it ultimately becomes self-contradictory. This raises the very legitimate question whether snobbery is not really a subtle form of asocial behaviour, which continually longs for approval although it spikes its own guns already in the basic act of fashion choice or lack of discrimination. In the texture of society the snob radiates a distinctly unhappy consciousness; no matter how hard he strives after social acceptance and to adapt himself to fashion by elevating it, as it were, to his religion, he always and inevitably fails in his efforts to enter the mainstream of society because he is always ahead of the current establishment. At the same time he has the peculiar urge to seek contact with the very people who reject him. His insecurity leaves him no other way out than to exaggerate. He thus becomes a true fop, in which he resembles the already mentioned elements on the fringe of society. Hence the snob can circulate only among certain types of society, those that have already passed through a strong process of individualization and exhibit a ready and marked mobility in fashion, which has, as it were, become their conventional canon of everyday life. In these social circles the snob truly represents a borderline case of fashion-oriented behaviour.

We must distinguish between snobbery and hobby, which is also usually strongly fashion-oriented. It serves above all to sustain a person when everyday life threatens to become bogged down too deeply in conventionalism. The hobby thus becomes a kind of safety valve which in an all-too-narrow confinement within an intolerant canon of respectability offers those concerned at least an illusion of freedom (as was the case, for instance, in Victorian England). Likewise the hobby can become an expression of escapism, whose main function consists in safeguarding the personal variant of life at least in a playful (non-economic) dimension. Exactly like snobbery, the hobby represents a borderline case of social and fashion-oriented behaviour.

It is significant that the snob, as we have already mentioned, practises uncritical imitation of the socially untried novelty, which has therefore not yet acquired any market value but remains quite outside the convention. In spite of his position on the fringe of society it frequently happens that other unstable elements in turn imitate the snob in a kind of vicarious and low form of snobbery, highly reminiscent of the feudal tenant who imitated his lord. This is where we usually find the origin of the so-called 'clique', which is a special form of small group within the framework of a larger society; led by a focal personality, it deliberately segregates itself from its environment and evolves its own ritual, which in the main cannot be socially transmitted. Thus the cliques, too, belong to the fringe groups, but with the distinguishing feature that the behaviour characterizing them is constructed (as in the snob) in a completely extra-social manner. The fact that the cliques, literary cliques for instance (which are responsible for many a fashion trend), often display this behaviour with a certain emphatic solemnity must not delude us that it is of importance to society as a whole. For the central value is, after all, only the result of a whim of snobbery and largely non-communicable. In other words it is a mark of distinction which is not acknowledged by the rest of society. Hence also the strongly esoteric character of most cliques.

These are, so to speak, the pure borderline cases in which imitation loses both its social justification (distinction) and its sociability-inducing function. In spite of the loudly professed solidarity of the clique (which has, however, mainly a negative basis, the rejection of the humdrum – *odi profanum vulgus et arceo* . . .) the members of the clique are fundamentally just as asocial as their chosen leader. Cliques are thus typical outsider groups. This is proved by, among other features, the fact that they are naturally short-lived, not only because they soon wither away, but also and mainly because they regularly and quickly disintegrate through internal dissension.

The clique is thus fundamentally a minor expression of asocial behaviour which temporarily assumes a solemn, lofty air of common purpose. But basically each of its members remains alone and apart from the others; after all, loneliness is not overcome by an exalted, indeed often hysterically eccentric etiquette. Hence also the trait of obtrusive human inadequacy that all too often characterizes sects of extreme philosophical views; it is associated with a slight hint of the ridiculous, of which the members are perhaps secretly aware but which merely confirms them even more in their position as outsiders because they are, after all, incapable of finding a normal approach to everyday society.

These remarks were necessary to show the strange deviations to which pure imitation can lead. In reality, however, it is an established fact that it can usually carry out its function only in already existing social circles; it is therefore an emanation of pre-existent social orders. Considered in isolation it signifies nothing at all. Within the framework of already existing social orders, however, it has the effect mainly of continuously activating and more richly developing such orders, of creating traditions and stimulating fashions. People imitate simply because social orders have the character of regimentation; but these social imperatives do not grow from imitation.

15 Ceremonial Behaviour and Etiquette

Fashion, then, appears increasingly as a special form of regulated behaviour. This peculiarity of fashion, already stressed at the beginning of our discussion, has meanwhile been more closely outlined on several occasions so that we are gradually enabled to give a more precise definition of fashion. To begin with it represents a more or less compulsive periodical change of style, as we were able to point out following some of S. R. Steinmetz's remarks. This change of style is in the last resort aided by a fundamental curiosity of the human race, regarded at the same time as a distinction and more and more enhanced by competition. Distinction depends on the approval of the spectators, just as competition is subject to firm rules which in our case are mainly concerned with ceremonial behaviour and the maintenance of a certain standard. Fashion began with the upper classes of the professional and aristocratic systems of antiquity and the Middle Ages, with the individual members and constituent groups of the upper stratum of society competing with one another and at first excluding the lower classes from it. We thus find fashion-oriented behaviour in the upper, folk costumes in the lower classes. We shall see later that, beginning with the changes of most social systems at the end of the Middle Ages (since the fourteenth and fifteenth centuries) to the democratic societies of the present day, the realm of fashion has steadily expanded. But its roots have not changed for all that; all we can note is the various styles of the social effects of fashion. But we must first further analyse the 'dictatorial' character of fashion so that we can understand why after the sudden and periodical change of style to which we have so far exclusively confined our discussion a period of stability occurs during which conformity to fashion becomes an obligation.

In step with the development of the basic social character of mankind in certain historic societies we find a formation of specific uniformities of behaviour. These begin with the simplest habits and customs and rapidly rise to the status of usage and law; as they do, not only does the mandatory character of these rules, but also the consciousness with which a certain behaviour is demanded become more and more marked. We are expected to observe customs simply because they are customs, without any further reason given. With usage the reason is already better defined: we follow usage because our ancestors have done so.

Finally, the law is based on the highest justification man knows, since it is regularly backed by religious forces, which are derived either directly from a divine law-giver or from a heroic figure formulating the law on behalf of a god. To this scale, which extends from casually observed habits to the ideas of justice, corresponds a differential formulation of the sanctions imposed if the rules are violated. In the simplest case, for instance, a deviation from a habit, the sanction will be very mild indeed; it will not go beyond slight disapproval, perhaps accompanied by ridicule. Transgression of the rules of custom and law invokes progressively more severe sanctions, ending with punishment.

Fashion, too, is part of this system of regimentation. Here one may also claim that it can be traced back to the profoundest depths of mankind. For an important root of fashion is the ceremonial behaviour *per se*, whose extraordinary significance in the development of human society was recognized at an early stage. Ceremonial behaviour simply says that with a given attitude it is not only the quality of the action, but also the way it is carried out that is decisive. In this sense the life even of primitive mankind is filled with innumerable ceremonial behaviour patterns, which in extreme cases may affect the whole existence of the community. With the higher development of mankind since the ancient advanced civilizations, ceremonial behaviour became not only more marked, but also subdivided into a number of more clearly circumscribed individual systems, such as the conventions, etiquette, respectability which ultimately helped to erect the whole edifice we call civilization. But this development always aims at taming the original instincts and driving forces of man and at making them amenable to higher forms of civilization. Inhibitions of a regulating character gradually create a second nature of man in which he appears above all as a socio-cultural person. This regimentation is passed on from generation to generation by means of education so that in time major and minor traditions build up, in which ultimately man is more at home than in his original animal nature. Seen in this light the entire process of historical development appears as a kind of self-domestication of mankind.

The immense variations of the ceremonial behaviour of mankind make any attempt at even vaguely outlining it quite impossible. Nevertheless we had to lay bare at least the basic features of this new root of fashion because this is the only way to demonstrate why the sudden change of style can assume a compulsive character. This root, too, however, branches into a large number of other phenomena so that the most diverse interconnections of fashion become evident here. In addition, this very attunement of fashion to man's general ceremonial behaviour makes the reason abundantly clear why in spite of its essential short-term nature fashion change may in certain conditions produce persistent forms of behaviour. These will then appear not only as firm customs but occasionally even as real 'cultural achievements' which in the end can no longer be divorced from man's cultural image, because they are psychologically 'fixed'.

The special form of ceremonial behaviour in our case is 'etiquette'. This means a ceremonial and conventional behaviour in certain situations, dictated more or less expressly by a society as a whole or in part (rank, class, profession) as the 'decent' behaviour in the sense of the preservation of a standard. Deviations from etiquette attract ridicule, laughter, and possibly even stronger forms of disapproval – up to boycott. It is a decisive quality of etiquette that it serves above all for the formulation of that intermediate layer of behaviour patterns situated halfway between ethics and aesthetics. It can thus have the effect of a general aesthetic 'varnish' of society, above all when it succeeds in gradually establishing itself over long periods of time. The classical example of this is perhaps the smile of the Chinese and the Japanese; this has developed into a veritable language, which at the same time expresses a central facet of culture as such. We have something analogous in the American 'keep smiling'. In spite of the essentially impersonal nature and debasement of such attitudes, it is still possible to use etiquette with sympathy and to modify it in the light of special situations. We then speak of 'tact' whose precise function is the individual modification of social rules.

No matter how fleeting etiquette may be and how weightless the attitudes and objects are to which it is attached, it, too, can assume a quasi-canonical character and become codified. Innumerable tracts exist on 'decorous' behaviour, that is, on the canon of reputability about which we have already spoken. Something similar is found in the 'books on good manners' of feudal Japan although this is less known. It is extremely significant that this kind of literature should appear especially in aristocratic and class-dominated societies, and that the words 'courteousness' and 'courtesy' should be derived from 'court'. But it is also part of this ceremonial behaviour of etiquette that it continually incorporates new ideas capable of providing human life with fresh stimuli. Thus ever new decorative forms of behaviour and the outward presentation of man are adopted in an almost experimental manner with the result that some of them will become part of the permanent inventory of civilization, whereas others disappear after varying periods of time. But they are never a merely superficial, mechanical imitation and automatic adaptation but mandatory behaviour in the strict sense.

16 The Process of Civilization and Modesty

Although etiquette is concerned mainly with the outward trappings of life it would be totally wrong to underrate its significance for the general structure of the socio-cultural personality of which the close relation between fashion-oriented behaviour and the sexual sphere is particularly strong evidence. Some time ago the Belgian J. P. Haesaert was able to show convincingly that in civilized humanity the feelings of revulsion have become stronger and stronger, so that punitive laws to deal with the exhibition of obscenity (exhibitionism) have become more and more severe, whereas primitive mankind was quite unconcerned in this respect. It seems that reactions to violations of public decency have become increasingly sensitive; naturally, this applies mainly to the social sphere but, as will be shown, in a wider sense also to the general aesthetic concepts of life into which the growing revulsion against the representation of sex has moved. Naturally we do not deny that certain individuals have known the feeling of revulsion from the beginning of time; but as a social phenomenon this feeling is extremely recent and did not occur before the advanced civilizations of antiquity. It is most relevant that these feelings were found mainly among the upper classes and in typical urban civilizations, which together offered the most important stage on which fashion could unfold. In this respect the lower classes lived much less restricted lives and enjoyed sometimes quite coarse amusements right down to our own days, as any superficial study of the history of morals will show. In the end modesty as we interpret it today appears purely as a product of civilization in that it increasingly generalizes the originally completely individual feeling and incorporates it in the canon of reputability. But we thereby concede that here fashion can play an important role in, for instance, dictating what parts of the body may be bared and what must be hidden so that the feeling of revulsion is not aroused.

We have already seen that the ornaments of primitive peoples not only do not hide, but on the contrary emphasize, the primary and secondary sexual characteristics; occasionally they even ostentatiously enlarge them. We find this tendency alive as late as the sixteenth century in the cod-piece of the mercenaries. With the increasing sensitivity, but above all the endeavour to draw an ever clearer dividing line against the coarse lower classes, more and more activities concerned with man's purely physical nature were carefully hidden; sometimes the display of one, sometimes of another part of the body caused revulsion (one merely needs to remember that not quite a century ago the display of a foot or an ankle by a woman was absolutely outrageous). Closer study of these problems, however, quickly reveals that almost all these behaviour patterns started as fashions. We must emphasize that fashion not only conceals, but occasionally also reveals, which at the same time affords curious evidence of the change in the spiritual climate of certain epochs. This particularly concerns the changing attitudes towards the female breasts, which were completely concealed at a very early stage, whereas the abdomen was strongly emphasized, for instance throughout the Middle Ages; with the introduction of the plunging neckline (the decolleté) at the end of the Middle Ages they were ostentatiously displayed. But here it could be said that the taming of the originally irresistible sex drive had, at least among the upper classes, already become a reality, so that this display was no longer felt as a direct provocation, but only as aesthetically tamed eroticism. This applied at least to the woman, whose sexual zone is not as directly localized and concentrated as the man's, so that from her point of view any form of erotic attraction is much more diffused, able to affect the whole body as it were; this also weakens its appeal considerably. The more or less ostentatious display of the breasts when the plunging neckline is the fashion is therefore felt to be provocative and correspondingly criticized mainly by men, but almost never by women. It may be of interest as a curiosity that the plunging neckline also existed for men, as the famous self-portrait by Albrecht Dürer of 1498 shows; but it was not generally accepted. Dürer also left many studies of the female plunging neckline, including even a Virgin Mary (1512).

This complex of problems, however, is by no means confined to the erotic sphere, but in practice affects all activities of the body and its needs. The progressive advance of the 'threshold of embarrassment' and the 'limit of modesty' is a general phenomenon, as Norbert Elias has been able to show in an extremely informative work, the *Process of Civilization*. This may determine the manner of eating and drinking, indeed table manners in general, spitting, sneezing, noseblowing, and innumerable other activities. We take certain behaviour patterns in all these situations so much for granted that we no longer appreciate that they first had to be acquired and shaped by society before the current canon could be established. But it is of decisive importance that, like most of our 'manners', they all started as definite fashions and genuine 'innovations'. This also implies that they first appeared in the upper strata of the system of the old estates and from there percolated through the whole of society during a process lasting many centuries, representing 'submerged cultural heritage'. This process developed the more rapidly the closer the relation of the other, especially the bourgeois, classes to the upper classes. We thus find in typically lower middle class civilizations, which within the estates system had not yet reached political, social, and economic self-expression, a strong resentment against not only anything related to fashion, but also any refined customs, which tend to be considered affected and were opposed with a deliberate 'naturalness'. This situation was of the greatest significance for the attitude of the German lower middle classes of the eighteenth century towards France and was still an underlying feature of the violently anti-French abuse of the German fashion historian Max von Boehn and the previously mentioned Friedrich Th. Vischer.

The decisive impulse towards the establishment of etiquette was provided by the knightly and courtly society of Provence and the neighbouring Italy: learned clerics, too, compiled canons of good manners (from the twelfth and thirteenth centuries on). The new spirit of courtly behaviour spread farther and farther afield from its countries of origin; with the rise of the guilds accompanying the great revolutions of the fourteenth and fifteenth centuries it also affected new social groups, about which we shall presently have more to say. In spite of all these developments it remains obvious, as Norbert Elias especially has shown, that these innovations of fashion express the self-confidence of the various groups constituting the medieval upper classes. All the nomenclature of this style of behaviour therefore points clearly in a certain social direction. Thus a special 'standard' is set up 'how to behave at court' (courtesy, *courtoisie, cortezia, hövescheit, Höflichkeit*). As we have previously mentioned, this did not, however, apply to knighthood as a whole, but only to the top group around the great feudal lords. Sometimes the new behaviour spread among wider circles, but at first never very far. Fashion competition largely remained confined to the top groups, which also implied the usual ostentatious display of extraordinary wealth. Thus objects and utensils such as knives, forks, and spoons used at table were made of specially selected precious material. Here wealth as such was still a mark of distinction which decided not only the owner's social rank, but also his position in the political hierarchy; at a later stage the rich, as Steinmetz correctly observed, no longer formed an estate, and even less a coherent group likely to become dominant.

This etiquette had the effect that medieval table manners for instance were slowly modified (originally meat was taken with the hands from a common plate, wine drunk from a common glass). There was also evidence of a general change in the emotional life of the people as it affected their social relations, as can be seen in the numerous treatises on manners published during the Renaissance and the Reformation, above all in an essay by Erasmus of Rotterdam (*De civilitate morum puerilium*), which was extraordinarily successful. He no longer presented the correct behaviour as a standard in a proverbial style, but already described what kind of behaviour people of his time expected of one another. We also notice that these rules of behaviour began to spread beyond the feudal upper class – the author himself was a member of the bourgeoisie and a classical scholar. One can generally claim that with the rise of the urban bourgeoisie and the humanist intellectuals the old feudalism had been severely weakened even before the system of princely absolutism reached the stage of its final development. That this was a typical time of transition can be seen from the fact that Erasmus mentioned without any inhibition certain physical needs and functions which later became unmentionable. At the same time the bourgeois intellectual acquired a strong self-confidence; the fact that he accepted his rules of behaviour no longer exclusively from the feudal upper class is ample proof of this. Thus the term 'courtesy' was relegated to the background and replaced by 'civility', which without doubt has more general applications; but as yet not general enough to be able to open up society as a whole to the fashion game; this was shown above all by the strong objection to the coarse manners of the lower classes, which has persisted right to our own days. It was thus possible for civility to retreat again, for the time being, to the upper classes of princely absolutism ('*le monde*'); only during the course of the nineteenth and twentieth centuries, after the general democratization of the western societies, did it develop into the current style of the social effects of fashion, which has to all intents and purposes captured the general public.

At that point it became decisive that fashion entered into a general reaction with already highly developed feelings of sensitivity, modesty, and embarrassment concerning certain human, all-too-human everyday functions. Innovations which served to calm these feelings, for instance our table manners and innumerable other psychologically fixed behaviour patterns, became a permanent part of civilized life; with only minor deviations they have become typical of the entire western world. How much consideration these feelings demanded is shown by the fact that they occasionally overcame even powerful inhibitions. One need only think of the introduction of the fork from Byzantium, which at first created a real scandal in Venice; the revulsion, with its profoundly religious basis, from the wearing of 'foreign apparel' and the acceptance of foreign habits may also have contributed to it. But on the other hand the use of the fork answered a strong need for improved manners in the top strata of society; from that time onwards it was mentioned without fail when an important personage had left several forks to his lucky heirs. In our age the use of this implement is a permanent feature of civilization.

Today the strongest feelings of revulsion are aroused by the performance in public of certain bodily functions, such as belching, breaking wind, urinating, and defaecating, at least in the Protestant civilizations north of the Alps; in southern Europe and elsewhere people are less sensitive in this respect. The most powerful stigma, however, is attached to the public performance of sexual intercourse, and even to some erotically significant gestures, whereas in the mediaeval bath houses there was much less prudery; among the upper classes, public performance of the nuptials was often an unavoidable duty.

17 The First Spread of Fashion-oriented Behaviour

The first style of the social effect of fashion within the upper ranks of the feudal system was soon followed by others, which were connected with the great social revolutions since the end of the Middle Ages. These led above all to an increasingly rapid dissolution of the old feudal system, which was confronted by the self-confident bourgeoisie of the cities. Only now do we find, as we have previously mentioned on several occasions, that imitation began to act from the bottom to the top, or that the middle classes demanded analogous distinctions, which had the direct result of speeding up the movement of fashion during this period. This also provoked the resistance of the feudal upper classes, and on the one hand sharpened the internal competition between the upper ranks of society; on the other hand attempts were made to control and effectively to counter by special dress regulations the increasing susceptibility to fashion of the city dwellers and their occasional positive ostentation.

Dress regulations and sumptuary laws are, of course, very old; we find them already in antiquity, where for instance the width of purple bands on official robes was laid down in minute detail. In 808 Charlemagne also promulgated regulations prescribing a person's dress according to his membership of a social class. Although we cannot judge today whether these regulations were successful, we are entitled to claim that a considerable increase of such ordinances suggests an increasing tendency towards their violation. We merely have to remember the observation that at the root of every taboo there must be a desire. During the thirteenth century, at the precise moment when the urban middle classes began to rise, there occurred indeed a sudden and steep increase in the number of dress regulations which have continued unabated ever since. In fact, the cities, too, soon began to join this countermovement after the ostentation of the burghers had threatened to get as much out of hand as that of the feudal lords. The success of this legislation can, incidentally, be judged with only a passing glance at the history of fashion: since the end of the fourteenth century an extraordinary versatility of the styles of dress suddenly emerged among all the upper classes simultaneously; in addition the many books on folk costumes written or drawn throughout Europe are clear evidence of the increasing interest large sections of the population took in these matters. The principal authors were, in chronological order, the Italian Enea Vico, Matthäus and Veit Konrad Schwarz of Augsburg, the Dutchman Abraham Bruyn, the Frenchman J. J. Boissard, the Swiss Jost Amman, the North German Heinrich Aldegrever; all their books were reprinted and imitated many times. This literature was instrumental in gradually reducing local fashions and setting the stage for a more European fashion; initially this development was rather arbitrary, in that everybody simply adopted anything he happened to see. The many voices thundering against the wearing of 'foreign apparel', like the prophets, in ancient Israel, remained unheard. An exuberant spring of fashion set in, which occasionally exhibited almost anarchical trends.

 This clearly reveals the connection between the breakdown of the estates system and the spread of fashion; but it is still open to question whether we may here speak of imitation in the strict sense. One sometimes gains the definite impression of a spontaneous eruption of a need for distinction in dress, underlined by the occurrence particularly among the various leading groups of the bourgeoisie of exactly the same spirit of competition as previously among the feudal nobility. This was evident especially in Italy and southern Germany where the great merchants soon adopted princely airs, whereas the old humanists and even the courtier Castiglione in vain castigated this trend. A significant pattern of this situation was the progress of Florence from the austerity of Cosimo de' Medici to the magnificence of Lorenzo.

It is not our task to examine the historical aspect of these various questions; this has already been done often enough. Our only concern is to emphasize certain principles which characterize this new style of social spread of fashion. We already know the most important innovation: the urban bourgeoisie began to exercise social power in its own right and was also prepared to fight for it in the social and political field, as shown by the insurrection of the Netherlands since the end of the sixteenth century, the English revolution of the seventeenth and the French revolution of the eighteenth century. In a word, the bourgeoisie rose forcefully from a lowly to a higher position, and did this in a way completely different from all such earlier attempts. At the same time a new system of government arose in the royal absolutism of England, Spain, and France, which was incomparably more strongly organized and centralized than the old feudal system. But since the Crown now made frequent use of the bourgeoisie to fight against the remaining great feudal lords, the feudal nobility was necessarily forced into direct competition with the bourgeoisie and a new aristocracy appointed from the ranks of government officials. This state of affairs became more and more acute since military service, originally the hereditary livelihood of the old feudal elements and the knights, became the absolute prerogative of the central government of the country. In practice there remained hardly any possibility now for the nobles to distinguish themselves in their own field; they became completely idle. Thus fashion and etiquette became the crucial means by which the aristocratic courtier could alone assert his position under the regime of absolutism.

Centuries passed before this situation was reached, but the consequences were nevertheless clearly visible. Hemmed in between central government and the rising bourgeoisie, the aristocracy of the absolutist period was compelled to draw a very sharp distinction between itself and the bourgeoisie to preserve its self-confidence. But since the bourgeoisie followed its every move, it was continually forced to devise new means of distinction to maintain the differential. Thus once again the rhythm of the movement of fashion was accelerated, the styles became transformed at ever shorter intervals. But this also meant that distinction and competition must assume more radical forms, since what was in the last resort involved was a struggle for power. This became all the more obvious to those it affected since this struggle for power was fought not only within the various nations but also on an international plane as soon as it was evident that the claim of the prerogative of power had passed from the imperial office to the office of the kings [in the context of the history of the Holy Roman Empire. The translator]. This initiated a number of wars, in which Spain, England, and France fought for hegemony in Europe.

Fashion, however, accompanies power. We can see this readily when we remember the chaos of fashions which spontaneously arose in all European countries at the end of the Middle Ages. Everybody adopted at random whatever ideas were offered to him. But at the very moment when Spain became a world power (under Emperor Charles V) Spanish fashion began to dominate; it was later replaced on the continent by the French. It is, incidentally, a significant aspect of this development that it proceeded independently of the great political controversies of the age. Thus Spanish costumes became the rage in England at the very moment when the country was involved in a life-and-death struggle with Spain.

What happened on an international plane was also reflected within the various societies; this reflection became the stronger the more the new court ceremonial developed and spread. Whereas at the Spanish Court the women still remained relatively in the background, their role under Louis XIV became so important that they began to dominate the entire picture of fashion. The influence of the prestige associated with power often created those abstruse, showy and pompous, as well as monstrous fashions of all kinds, which, because of their extravagant character, were the rage often for no longer than a few months, but on account of their followers' high rank have been preserved for us in countless illustrations. The compulsion to which the court aristocracy was subjected to keep aloof, in the interest of its self-assertion, from anything 'bourgeois' and 'common' necessarily led to increasing artificiality, which was reflected by no means in dress alone, but also in the entire style of life, the deportment, and the manner of speaking and ultimately even of thinking. The fact that the aristocrats had now become strictly a 'leisured class' (according to Thorstein Veblen), whose entire aspirations were confined to the development of a refined style of life, further reinforced this trend. This also offered opportunities to adopt foreign ideas from the most distant parts of the world; the Far Eastern (Chinese and Indian) influences on the French aristocracy established this trend as early as the seventeenth century.

Although the aristocracy was now permanently locked in competition with the bourgeoisie, it is necessary to record that the Ancien Régime persisted up to 1789 unopposed at least on the European continent (with the important exceptions of Switzerland and the Netherlands). Although the court fashions did spread as a result, this spread was by and large rather limited because the lower classes, after all, were not very familiar with the appropriate ceremonial. Distinct from this was the development of real 'fancy fashions' by certain groups such as the mercenary soldiers from the fifteenth and sixteenth centuries on (the 'slit costume'). Events had made these mercenaries extraordinarily mobile and their craving for distinction caused them to employ the most unusual means to flaunt themselves before the astonished eyes of the peasants and burghers. The Swiss draughtsman Urs Graf immortalized in masterly, violent, passionate strokes these itinerant folk on the fringe of society. Whereas the pompous, showy dress of the aristocracy strikes us as frigid, hiding any personal impulse behind rigid ceremonial, the fancy fashions of the mercenaries often displayed childish enjoyment of the bizarre. The main purpose was to catch the eye, and the soldiers were therefore often represented by the artist in a way that left the decision to the viewers whether he took his subject quite seriously or merely caricatured it.

It is significant that this caricaturist style was applied mainly to men and male fashions; its chief function was to bring out the 'coxcomb' parading his manhood; the Latin Americans even invented a special expression for this: they speak of 'machismo'. We find no analogies to this with women, especially young women; at most they are shown to be quite undeterred from squeezing into an ugly uniform provided it happens to be fashionable. The 'vamp', which corresponds to the 'coxcomb', on the other hand, has no comical connotations.

The fact remains that fashion accompanies power. Since power was at first – although not undisputedly – in the hands of absolute monarchs and the court aristocrats, this situation persisted up to 1789, in spite of the fact that the bourgeois classes were taking over one position after the other. But their only chance of survival was to move closer to the aristocracy, which was already proof that the old system had long been decaying from within. For from that point onwards absolutism largely used the middle classes in order to retain its grip on the state, whereas the pomp and circumstance of absolutism in

15. Juliette Greco in a black jumper; she revolutionized the fashion of young women in the immediate post-war years. *dpa*

16. An admirer takes leave kissing the lady's hand (after Moreau de Jeune, 1777). *Staatsbibliothek Berlin*

time ruined the aristocracy completely except those of its members who succeeded in marrying their sons to the daughters of the 'bourgeois gentilhomme', thereby giving fresh lustre to their somewhat faded coats of arms. But this was already life at second hand.

18 Fashion in the Bourgeois Moneyed Circles

We have now arrived at a stage when another style of social spread of fashion developed; it is the beginning of what is still dominant in our own days. It originated in the total collapse of the estates system, absolutism, and its aristocracy. But that this turn of events since the French revolution initiated another speed-up of fashion change, which is still in full swing today, is in itself proof of the tenuousness of the basic connection between fashion and the estates system. From now on, however, the many strands of fashion motivation appear in full view, a motivation which not only adopts concrete impulses from everywhere but at the same time aligns itself with a large number of principles of which we already know some, and shall shortly discover others. The character of fashion increasingly proves to be a universal formative principle of society, acquiring a downright tyrannical control over social development, with modern economy an ally of truly inexhaustible resources. We must, however, stress already at this stage that, without the previously traced primeval roots of fashion, economic development alone could never have produced this flowering. A certain disposition existed, to which was added the historical experience and habituation in the development of a special life style. But now fashion began to enjoy the support of undreamt-of technical and economic facilities and of a peculiar social constitution, so that the original germ was suddenly assisted by the most unlikely possibilities of development. Yet it cannot be claimed that these possibilities were created by the economy alone.

But we must approach this stage step by step if we are not to neglect the considerable number of intermediate phases between the French revolution and our own era. We must above all remember that the old estates and aristocracies did not disappear at a stroke and that there existed various currents which aimed at a restoration of pre-revolutionary conditions. On the contrary, they underwent a very peculiar transformation during the time immediately following their fall from political power, which provided fashion and the way it spread through society with most potent impulses. When power disintegrates, it does not suddenly leave a complete vacuum; in fact there is the chance of a strangely unreal and occasionally truly ghostlike afterlife, which we call 'prestige'. This may in certain conditions shine the more brightly the more remote it is from reality; a striking example is the idea of the system of estates and the mediaeval empire during the age of German Romanticism. To this we must add the diehards constantly hankering after 'the good old days'. We thus witness the intriguing spectacle that the bourgeoisie – after all the spontaneous creative fashion feats it had accomplished since the end of the Middle Ages – slavishly imitated the old aristocracy at the precise moment when this had definitely lost all its power. A strange paradox, which once again shows up the limitations of the theory of imitation in fashion change. It must moreover be borne in mind that one can speak less and less of a fashion change that was induced by the lower imitating the upper classes. For aristocracy, shorn of its power, progressively lost the means of distinguishing itself from the advancing middle classes. But this is followed by a very strange imitation of the aristocratic system as a whole by the bourgeois class. Thus the bourgeois class system of the nineteenth century became established, which, as we know today, even if it is not apparent at first glance, drew substance to a far greater extent than was at first realized from the leftovers of the old estates system. One can even say that originally the middle-class industrial society arose with the emphasis on having overcome all the prejudices of the Ancien Régime. How little this is true, especially as regards fashion, was shown by Edmond Goblot in an extremely witty little book that already provided us with the terms 'barrier' and 'standard'. He summarized the whole problem in a single sentence: 'what distinguishes the bourgeois is distinction itself.' He thereby clearly equated distinction or rank with exclusiveness, conceding the bourgeoisie of the beginning of the nineteenth century exactly the same position as the court aristocracy previously enjoyed. It was therefore not the fashion content which was imitated, but the fashion-based exclusiveness, with the aid of etiquette and ceremonial. Only now can we see the classical picture of a class society in which the upper class scrupulously avoided too close vicinity with the others and the experience of unexpected contacts with them. Hence the significant synonym for 'bad' company: a 'mixed crowd'. A mixed crowd is one in which we are not 'among ourselves'. All these, however, are the typical manifestations of aristocratic exclusiveness which were simply copied here in their entirety. To us they appear a little musty although we have not left them all that far behind.

At the beginning of the bourgeois era we thus find the emphasis on the segregation of the 'people of quality' from all the rest. Accordingly many old phrases were adopted, such as the French *je vais dans le monde* to express a liking for social life. But *le monde* was originally identical with the exclusive world, jealously guarded against intruders, of the aristocracy, which cultivated the 'correct' tone in all walks of life as its most precious privilege. And from this borrowed platform attempts are made to represent even certain fringe manifestations of modern society as a function of that long abandoned '*monde*' by calling them '*demimonde*'. This procedure, incidentally, corresponds exactly to the usage that attempts to describe the old world and the new in the same terms by calling for instance the modern wage labourers and the 'proletariat' of the beginning of the nineteenth century the 'fourth estate' unaware of the fact that the existence of wage labourers and the proletariat, parts in fact of the completely different post-revolutionary class system, had destroyed any proper estates system. But estates and classes are not the same, no matter how much the top group of the new bourgeoisie at the beginning of the nineteenth century sought, but its behaviour, to act as the successor of the old aristocracy.

The tendency of distinction of the bourgeois upper class now spread to life as a whole. Everything was 'first', 'second', 'third' class: on the railways and the seats in the theatre. But the distinctive mark was no longer the 'standard' of behaviour, but simply price, which suddenly established wealth with its typical inexorable laws as the true arbiter of life styles. We must stress that even now this attitude is of extraordinary importance particularly among literary circles: in Great Britain, for instance, novels first appear as hardcovers, bought by the affluent and trendy connoisseurs; after a decent interval the hardcover is followed by the 'popular' paperback edition. The French, too, are familar with this system, but there it has a different function since the cheap and the various expensive luxury editions are published simultaneously; the average result is that a reader who has enjoyed a book in the cheap edition buys the more expensive edition to place on his bookshelf. Without doubt purely monetary considerations and snobbery have their effect also in France; nevertheless the exclusively artistic approach to the book and its corresponding valuation still survive. Phenomena of this kind, however, often mask the importance of the new wealth of the industrial society, a wealth which can be acquired in the most varied ways (as Balzac's novels show), so that the rich form no group apart. In the estates and aristocratic order, on the other hand, a characteristic style, a specific etiquette stood at the beginning;

the display of wealth was a secondary manifestation associated with it. Naturally the survival of a purely feudalistic spirit and the establishment of a distinct 'moneyed aristocracy' was independent of this; some families successfully survived from the beginning of the nineteenth century to the present and developed a kind of life style which was based on their economic position at the top. By the very nature of the situation this group is small indeed.

Basically the only way to distinction left to the new bourgeoisie was segregation, for according to the law which established it differences of birth, the distinguishing mark of the aristocrats, were abolished. The bourgeoisie thus had to place artificial emphasis on the distance separating it from the rest. This created a peculiar paradox: the contempt of the masses which characterized already the Ancien Régime was once again reinforced after the masses had seized power. Fashion-oriented behaviour now became a definite necessity of life; at the same time it provoked the rivalry of the others. For where material wealth is the only distinguishing mark, the barrier is only low; you cannot acquire the status of birth; you can acquire money. From the beginning of the nineteenth century the social and economic advance of large numbers of people, too, was caused by the system of the industrial society and the 'leaders of society' were constantly spurred to change the fashion because many other groups were following hot on their heels.

Under this pressure a new canon of reputability was formed; it is by no means simple to describe it since we no longer have the origin by birth as the first mark of distinction. In fact the main emphasis was now on etiquette alone, which had to establish itself without tradition since the bourgeoisie of the industrial society was largely recruited from groups vastly different from that of the old city merchants. The regulation of fashion-oriented behaviour accordingly became extremely difficult. The representatives of the new bourgeoisie were torn between yesterday and tomorrow without the support of a

Fashion in the Bourgeois Moneyed Circles 151

tradition of their own which could tell them with certainty how one has to behave today. In other words, it was impossible to dress either in yesterday's or in tomorrow's fashion. The fashion of yesterday became popular and therefore 'commonplace'. The fashion of tomorrow was left to the fop, who was half admired, half despised. The question of the 'fashion novelty' therefore developed into a real problem. For the fashion-conscious member of the middle class, while always alert for what was 'new', could nevertheless not adopt a fashion the moment it appeared because if he immediately took up every idea he would be unconventional. Unconventionality violates the canon of reputability; he must adapt himself, remain inconspicuous and, if at all possible, live by the general code of conduct of his group. It is thus surprising to learn that the bourgeoisie of the nineteenth century was inherently unproductive in the realm of fashion. It was completely lost without examples to guide it. This leads us to a new principle of the spread of fashion, the setting of fashion trends; it was the trend setter who was now strictly imitated. But since the court aristocracy could no longer be directly imitated (although something of this still survived too) one wonders where the leaders of bourgeois society could look for their examples.

If we follow the new canon the examples can only be those persons who were not afraid of being conspicuous. These were the fops, the dandies, the swells, the *incroyables* and *merveilleuses*, in short, a fair section of society's outsiders as well as actors and actresses and the representatives of the *demimonde*, which played an important role especially in France. The bourgeoisie accepted these fashions as soon as they were no longer conspicuous but still distinctive. The dominant movement was quite clearly towards the avoidance of all extremes. The motto was the *juste milieu*. Thus what was new gradually became the fashion after it had lost its rough edges. It was considered refined, in other words distinguished and distinguishing, once it was no longer eccentric. And so the appearance of the real 'pioneers of fashion' who demonstrated it to the rest was decisive for the new way of spreading fashion. Here the great break with tradition that had come with the French revolution is revealed: innovations no longer develop from the canon handed down from the past, but are sometimes so new that they upset all customs. This was particularly obvious immediately after the Revolution when on the one hand long trousers became fashionable for men ('sansculottism'), and on the other the fashion of the chemise, so typical of the First Empire, became dominant among the women. As can be expected, this break with tradition resulted in great uncertainty in the creation of fashions: experiments were carried out more or less deliberately, with the appearance of many abortive fashions – which need not surprise the observer in view of the examples in this field. But at the same time another hitherto unknown personality appeared, the *créateur*, the fashion designer proper who leads his well planned expeditions into no-man's-land to offer the public a never-ending stream of novelties. He derives his ideas from the most unlikely quarters; from now on the purely external influences increase more and more; they can be traced only with a sound background knowledge of the contemporary history of morals. At the same time a kind of historical spirit began to influence the creations of fashion, based on a deliberate study of older fashions from which ideas for the present were adopted. This 'historicizing' spirit of fashion design seems to us to occur above all during periods of transition, when experimenting with ideas from the past becomes popular. In very recent times even men's fashions have become affected by it. These movements of fashion revival often receive their impulses from great distances both in time and space. Thus girl students at American colleges adopted the Mexican poncho (*quesquemetl*), which was immediately exported to Europe; the same applied to the American Indian fringed suede jackets.

To recapitulate: the upper ranks of the bourgeoisie adopted

their fashions from the fashion leaders when they were no longer quite new and had already lost their rough edges, so that 'the wearer does not become conspicuous'. But it was inevitable that fashion spread farther and farther since to adapt themselves the middle classes, who were rapidly gaining power and influence, very quickly imitated any characteristic of their social superiors. But this had also the effect that the upper classes could wear a fashion only as long as it was not too old. This brings us again face to face with the double function of fashion, demonstrated mainly by Goblot. Fashion is first a barrier; a movable one, it is true, but a barrier nevertheless which can only be surmounted with difficulty. On the other hand, fashion also establishes a standard. Although a fashion is changed quickly once it is no longer the preserve of a small leading group, it is also accepted only after it has been found capable of setting a standard. For while it is crucial that a fashion should not be readily available to everybody outside one's own privileged circle, it must nevertheless be able to ensure the distinction not only of the individual wearer, but of the entire class. This at least was the situation during the nineteenth century, and it has some after-effects even today. But additional problems have now arisen since the replacement of the class problems that existed during the nineteenth century by a completely new social structure.

The statement that the main object of fashion is to distinguish an entire class also indicates that the purely personal taste can affect only detail, never the general line. Taste is an individual matter, fashion a barrier between classes. Taste can accordingly affect only the way a person wears a fashion, never his choice of it. As long as fashion is a means of class differentiation it must protect the wearer not only from becoming ordinary but also from being too much transformed by personal modification. The eccentric is the death of fashion, but so is the aesthete, who has a very distinct personal taste. This is the last vestige of court etiquette.

19 Male Puritanism Versus Female Fashion

We have repeatedly seen that fashion is always an integral part not only of particular social constitutions, but also of certain cultural horizons. To be able to assess the full significance of these observations we must once again review the comprehensive cultural transformations that have taken place since the Reformation and the Renaissance, and above all since the replacement of the old order of feudalism and absolutism with the bourgeois industrial society. For these resulted in a well-defined shift of emphasis in fashion, especially regarding the different roles of the male and the female in the process of fashion change.

Thus, close relations exist, for instance, between the old feudalism, absolutism and patriarchalism. This is why in such an environment it was almost exclusively the men who wore the marks of distinction and fashions, whereas the women were sometimes strongly relegated to the background; if they did make an appearance, it was mostly only in a representative function (for example, as queens or as kings' mistresses). This applied particularly to the Renaissance: beyond the typical court life in Provence and Burgundy women were after the end of the Middle Ages subject to the greatest restraint. This situation, however, extended only partly to the urban patricians and the Italian Renaissance; the Spanish fashions provided the most striking evidence of female restraint.

We should like to point out in this context that this attitude

Male Puritanism Versus Female Fashion

is to some extent favoured by a clearly innate human trait: in the primitive world the male quite unmistakably exhibits a much greater need to adorn himself than the female. This closely resembles the situation in the animal kingdom where the males are distinguished by gorgeous plumage, gaudier colours, striking antlers and so on and are usually (though not always) larger than the females. As we approach the present this tendency in humans changes progressively: male fashions become more and more restrained, whereas female fashions unfold more and more fancifully. This remarkable change must have a reason that is deeply rooted in the structure of modern cultural awareness; it would otherwise have been incapable of inverting, as it were, the 'natural' order.

This new style of real austerity in male fashions first appeared at the Spanish Court, during the absolutist era when the ceremonial was like a strait jacket; the faces of the kings and their families look almost ghostlike, unreal to us. Here we have the strange phenomenon that the great antagonist of the Spanish monarchy, protestantism, faithfully copied its archenemy at least in this respect; at the height of the war Spanish fashions appear in England and the insurgent Netherlands. Fundamentally this is in line with a frequent observation that often Jesuitism and radical Calvinism become as like as two peas in a pod, at least as far as the severity of discipline ruling a person's whole life is concerned. Thus the dark colours, above all black, reached the Calvinist burghers of the Netherlands and the puritans in England from Spain, as Richard Alewyn has shown most compellingly:

> Long before Charles V retreated to the monastic community of S. Just he dressed in black, which on Titian's portrait eerily surrounds the emperor's tired, suspicious expression. At the beginning of the Baroque Age the colour of death dominated the dress of Europe's society. It occupied this position so long as Spain ruled the fashion. Its elegance was

cooler, more restrained than the irrepressible riot of colours of the Renaissance that corresponded to the new image of the courtier. Black thus frames the aloof, almost frozen faces portrayed by the Mannerists. Black, however, is also the natural expression of the new pessimism that spread through the world, beginning with the melancholy of the aging Michelangelo, the aging Shakespeare and mounting to the furious eruptions of world hatred and world-fear with which zealots and penitents destroyed the beautiful style of the Renaissance. Life is not worth the effort, man is a living corpse, the world a place of mourning – it was pronounced from all the pulpits. Small wonder that all the world dressed in the colour of mourning. The realm of black spread beyond the courts. Hardly ever was an idea of fashion so completely accepted by the bourgeoisie and so faithfully preserved. To the world-hating pathos of the Protestants and the practical sense of the bourgeoisie the lively colours, the scintillating velvet and silk garments were a godless abomination. The Huguenots in France, the Puritans in England were known by the dark, dull clothes they dressed in. And wherever the burghers reigned, from the nobili in Venice to the regents in Amsterdam, they reigned in black. The Dutch added to the dead black of the festive garments the sober white of clean linen. Dressed in the colours of seriousness and cleanliness the Dutch patricians are immortalized in the paintings of the regents by Rembrandt and Frans Hals. This colour scale – the subdued hues of wool and cotton colours for everyday wear, the abstract black and white for official occasions – has remained the basis of men's fashions throughout the bourgeois era. Only where the nobility succeeded in preserving its social domain and in diplomatic and military circles did the old, cheerful colours survive. They have been restored to society after the intermezzo of black, although not in their old artlessness.'

Since the reformation, which in more than one respect was the first great political self-assertion of the bourgeois world, but above all within the orbit of aggressive Calvinism we find from the very beginning a strong aversion to the ostentation and etiquette of the courts as well as to all luxury and extravagance, which were replaced by a demand for thrift. Thus a new fashion of sobriety and modesty for both men and women appeared, also in strong contrast with the ostentation of the urban population in the countries that had remained Roman Catholic – a difference which in fact is noticeable even today: gay colours are more prevalent among men and women in Italy, Spain, and South America than, for instance, north of the Alps. This Calvinistic, restrained fashion, which arrived in North America in the *Mayflower*, developed from a temporary fashion to a characteristic mark of style, particularly in men's dress. The man's suit of today is fundamentally a direct descendant of the puritan dress and thus still a political demonstration against the ostentation of the courts. It is no accident that England, the birthplace of rampant puritanism, has retained the leadership in men's fashions to our days, whereas Paris, which remained unaffected by the Reformation and was forcibly returned to the Roman Catholic faith by, of all people, a Florentine, Catherine de' Medici, during St Bartholomew's Night has been the centre for ladies' fashions ever since women gained dominant positions in France during the era of absolutism. This is where France differs both from Spain and England.

After the profoundly male puritanical ethos had not only prepared the world for the modern style of economy but, in the Cromwellian revolution of 1649, also administered the first decisive shock to the Ancien Régime, the political stage was set for the Puritans to steer the course of the new development. We can indeed observe a continuous line from these events to our own era, a line which becomes progressively more distinct as we approach the present. In Protestant countries even today men may change their fashions only within the narrowest limits (concerning minor items such as tie, fancy handkerchief, shoes, socks). In contrast, of Roman Catholic countries only France – which in spite of St Bartholomew's Night has been influenced more profoundly by the Huguenot spirit than is commonly appreciated – also adopted the sober men's fashion, adding to it the long trousers. The other countries of the reformation followed this trend, until at last the Roman Catholic countries, too, adapted themselves to the new economic order and accepted the new fashion.

But woman's attitude differs radically from man's. To begin with her fashions, too, became simpler in reformed circles. But parallel to it developed a relaxation of the old patriarchalism, which was gradually replaced – at first also in puritan England – by greater equality, most intimately connected with the emancipation of the middle classes. This was, however, only a beginning, of which consequences would not be felt until after the French revolution. For the time being the pressure of religious rules induced women to observe the greatest simplicity. But although economic attitudes were originally very largely determined by Calvinist ethics – in spite of the fact that some phenomena, especially the modern monetary system, had already developed in the Middle Ages – the increasing secularization of life as a whole brought about very radical changes in the situation after the middle of the eighteenth century. Economic attitudes became based increasingly on life in this world until they clearly gained the upper hand. The bourgeois class society unfolded parallel to this development, and a new style of social spread of fashion was created. This was a strangely new phenomenon in that it mainly affected women, whereas men's fashions, apart from a few minor changes, crystallized into a kind of permanent form. Men have thus stagnated in their fashions to this day.

Thorstein Veblen has pointed out that during the nineteenth century men largely broke with the traditional connection with the court aristocracy; not so the women, who in fact displayed a very curious attitude towards fashion: a number of trends were already appearing which have become significant for the popular democracies of the twentieth century. This fact, by the way, has had the greatest economic consequences. Since the vast majority of women enter the market as consumers, this curious attitude towards fashion cannot but affect the economy as a whole. Accordingly the change in the female attitude towards fashion cannot be overestimated. In contrast with the relatively constant men's fashions, women's fashions exhibit an extraordinary mobility so that in certain conditions they can change every season. Nor does this apply to detail only; occasionally it affects the general line, which often changes in a truly adventurous manner. The term 'New Look' is a very useful general term to denote this development (beyond its special association with fashion); for what changes is not only a secondary attribute, but appearance as a whole. It has already been shown how the bourgeois upper classes, stimulated by certain examples, began the change, with the middle classes gradually catching up with them. In this process the speed at which the woman caught up was quite remarkable. Woman has been fundamentally the perfect democrat from the moment she entered history on equal terms. She does not tolerate any distinction between the various classes. What the rich woman buys today will be cheaply copied tomorrow. And since the introduction of ready-to-wear fashions it has been found that the clothing industry can afford very little delay (often no more than a few weeks) after the fashion shows of the Haute Couture, because the female consumers of all classes instantly adopt the new line. This phenomenon is of extraordinary economic importance because it is not only the small upper class that reacts in this manner, but almost the entire female population, including the working women.

At first, however, the vast majority of the workers in the nineteenth century were men, the women entering working life only at a later stage. At the beginning of the century the quasifeudalistic fashion competition was joined mainly by the representatives of the upper classes, but this attitude spread with incredible speed to almost the entire female population so that in the end a completely new style of social spread of fashion was evolved, which by and large is still with us. Before this stage was reached, however, revolutionary changes took place in the world of women, which we must appreciate if we want to measure the distance that separates the situation today from the one prevailing at that period. Whereas the middle-class man knew only the ethics of working for a living and despised the leisure of the old aristocracy, women at the beginning of the century enjoyed leisure as social representatives of their husbands. This became, of course, possible only after the champions of the new style of economy had begun to amass some wealth, which made the position of a middle-class wife extraordinarily like that of the aristocratic counterpart. At the same time this was an entirely new situation; for until then a middle-class wife had played a regular role in the economic process, except that she carried out her work inside instead of outside the home. The lady of leisure of the middle classes is therefore a comparatively recent as well as transient phenomenon.

With the adoption of the aristocratic way of life, ostentatious consumption necessarily became a function of the women once a certain wealth had been acquired; for the survival of the old ideas and the new political atmosphere barred men from this activity. Fashion thus became a privilege of women, who, as a result, emphasized their sexual attraction in a completely new, hitherto unknown, manner. But since ostentatious consumption is an expression of power, competition again raised its head, except that it was no longer the men who were rivals in fashion: they conferred this task upon their wives while they pursued their careers. Work and money as well as personal thrift and the amassing of wealth played the chief parts in a man's life; money, however, was not spent on

17. Full-length evening gown by Balenciaga, Spring 1957
Modebuch Verlagsgesellschaft, Zürich

18. See-through fashions by Mary Quant, 1969. *Camera Press*

consumption, but above all reinvested. On the female side of society, among the upper classes at least, there was disdain of the eternal treadmill of work and money. One boasted of not doing any work; the hand was worshipped that never became dirty from menial tasks (as an unmistakable symbol of his contempt of menial work the Chinese mandarin grew his fingernails so long that he could not possibly use his hands).

We thus have the nineteenth-century ideal of the 'lady', enthroned upon a high pedestal, never touching the gound with her feet, and, as her husband's representative, executing the function of ostentatious consumption. The German philosopher Arthur Schopenhauer lashed out with venom at this 'excessive worship of the lady' at which, he said, not only the whole of Asia laughed, but the ancient Greeks and Romans would have laughed too. He continued with biting disapproval:

> For it is the power of reason which enables man, unlike the animals which live only in the present, to survey and assess the past and the future; it is the source of his caution, his worry, and his frequent apprehension. Woman is less affected by the advantages and disadvantages inherent in this situation because of her weaker intellect; in fact she is intellectually myopic, because her intuitive reasoning is occupied only with immediate concerns; its field of vision is narrow and excludes remote matters; this is why women are far less affected than we by anything absent, past, or future; one of the reasons for the tendency towards extravagance, found far more frequently with them and sometimes bordering on madness. Wives think in their hearts that it is the function of husbands to earn money, and theirs to squander it; if possible in their lifetime, and at least after the husband's death.

These sentiments need no comment. One could at best add that Schopenhauer is wrong if he means this to be a general characterization of all women; what he says refers only to the 'lady' of the middle-class economic order of the nineteenth century.

This lady, however, did not live in seclusion; she needed not only company, but also the male spectator for her fashion display. Her husband could not be cast in this role because he was busy without let-up in his factory and office, developing the system of the new economy until with the 'world market' he had reached the limits of expansion. The wife thus looked for a substitute and it did not take her long to find him. The substitute was the dandy or, as we would call him today, the playboy. The dandy lived on what was left to him from the feudal age; small wonder that the concept originated in England (where feudalism had persisted even during the industrial revolution), from where since 1815 it spread gradually across the whole of Europe. At the same time the dandy adopted elements of the feminine style; this created a very peculiar cultural atmosphere of a feminine nature in which the roles of man and woman were reversed; the man no longer courted the woman as in the past; the woman mirrored herself in the eyes of certain men to enjoy her own beauty narcissistically and to increase her self-confidence. It is extremely significant to note how the dandy adopted more and more Italian elements in his dress to move farther and farther away from the world of the middle classes. It is just as significant that these elements should have been drawn from one of the very countries that had rejected all reforms and had also to be regarded as industrially backward at the time. The dandy was then confronted with the, usually reformed, pioneer of modern industrial economy, who soberly got on with his work. Beau Brummell was the extreme representative of dandyism; he lived from 1778 to 1840 and was George IV's companion and *arbiter elegantiarum;* but he died in the poor house at Caen after fleeing from his creditors at home. He was followed by the representatives of the *jeunesse dorée,* who also paraded in front of the ladies of leisure while the husbands and fathers were busy earning money. Benjamin Disraeli represented a peculiar intermediate type: as a young man he was a perfect fop and dandy, but as a grown-up the proponent of sober capitalist imperialism, creator of the modern British Empire and faithful servant of his Queen Victoria with her prudish lack of imagination.

This style of civilization reached its end in Europe with the establishment, about 1850, of the new era of naturalism, which was entirely the result of the industrial revolution. The radical social criticism of naturalism brought about a profound disenchantment with the lady's and the dandy's romantic world, although this world was yet to experience a very strange transfiguration in the historical farce of Napoleon III's Second Empire, which, however, collapsed before the onslaught of the German armies in 1870. The purest exponent of this transitional period was Jacques Offenbach (1819–1880), whose star, significantly, was dimmed suddenly after 1870. The mirror in which the society of the Second Empire saw itself reflected was the operetta, which was a stage for all the characters we have just described. The operetta also became an important platform on which the new fashions developed, soon to be adopted by the ladies of leisure and their dandies. This was also the period of the French comedy of the Eternal Triangle: Eugène Scribe (1791–1861) was the unequalled master of this genre, who drew his points largely from the fact that the husbands work hard during the day, while their wives squander the hard-earned money with members of the *jeunesse dorée* and in the process treat the laws of marital fidelity with some levity. Alexandre Dumas-Fils (1824–95) represented the end of this epoch; with the same skill as Scribe he castigated the old Eternal-Triangle plays, although as a young man he had himself been the prototype of the late romantic era and panegyrist of the demi-monde, to which he erected an incomparable monument in his *La Dame aux Camélias*. Naturalism meant the complete disappearance of this world, which on the one hand suffused life with a fascinating glow, but on the other seems totally and disquietingly strange to us today.

But we must add in all fairness that the fashion creations of that epoch are of the greatest importance for the present in at least one respect: certain basic traits still survive unchanged, such as the Paris cafés, brasseries and restaurants, which still have the mirrored walls of the Second Empire reflecting an illusionist world of fantasy. Furthermore the shift of the impact of the fashion game, which is now in the hands of the women, has had extremely far-reaching consequences in that it has largely been responsible for the creation of a middle class style of interior decoration in the nineteenth century. This, too, partly drew on the feudalistic heritage: one has merely to remember the cheap horrors of the mass-produced Louis XV–Louis XVI or Empire style with its spindly-legged, stiff little chairs and the clumsy marble fireplaces. At the same time, women created the basis for an 'intimate' style of interior decoration, the modern, middle-class style of the *intérieur*. Interior decoration was unknown to the petty bourgeoisie of the seventeenth and eighteenth centuries, and although the city patricians of the preceding epoch created very distinct styles, these were confined to representative rooms and did not embellish private apartments. This advance was an achievement typical of the nineteenth century.

We can therefore claim that the total change of interior style corresponds to the development of the modern family with its strong need for privacy. The large halls of earlier ages were given up more and more in favour of small rooms, which also permit more and more differentiated interior decoration. Even works of art were adapted to this new style, the giant statues and outsize oil paintings of the past, measured in nothing less than square yards, disappeared to be replaced by works of small dimensions and an abundance of small knick-knacks, products of modern commercial art.

20 Fashion Captures the Masses

In spite of the all-pervading feudalistic pretensions of the industrial middle classes of the first half of the nineteenth century, which, naturally, still survive in certain quarters even today, the latest style of social expansion of fashion which still dominates the present age had its origin there. Naturally, several new (mainly economical) influences made themselves felt, but by and large it was the women who affected it to a quite extraordinary extent; the development of the egalitarian democracies, in which the old class system was slowly but surely eroded, further enhanced these effects. For in spite of all the political demands nobody was able to prevent the women from adopting the ever new fashions of the upper classes, so that uniformity was established with the greatest speed during each change of fashion. The rhythm of fashion development therefore had to become faster and faster, until it began in fact to move in a yearly cycle and only the general line survived longer than a year. This development was further supported by the establishment of industrial mass production of ready-to-wear clothes; in addition, the rapidly expanding consumer industries made the design of more and more products of everyday use subject to fashion, products within reach even of the less affluent sections of society. Thus the great masses gradually moved into the orbit of fashion consumption, which in the past had been generally closed to them.

That fashion has been able to spread to such a large sector

of the public is, however, the result of a novel, very fundamental change in our entire social system. The old estates had disappeared; so had absolutism; they were followed by the bourgeois class society of the beginning of the nineteenth century. Obviously this does not imply that all these old orders disappeared without a trace; much of them survives even today in the most varied sections of our society. We can therefore claim that all the mainsprings of fashion so far described are still functioning; a number of others, some established in the past, others completely new, such as the consumer industries, have been added to them. As a result, the motifs in the polyphony of fashion become more and more diverse; it accordingly becomes extremely difficult if not impossible to trace the extraordinarily complex phenomenon of fashion to a single root.

One trait characteristic of present-day society favours this remarkable acceleration of fashion development: its so-called 'social mobility'. This means that society is fluid, rid of all barriers of class and estate, and in an extraordinary state of flux – inwardly as well as outwardly. Today hardly anybody or any group any longer occupies stations in society pre-ordained by fate; people continually change their positions both horizontally (increase of travelling as well as of man's disposition to travel) and vertically, where a continual social rise and fall in the lives of individuals as well as of generations has destroyed all rigid estates and class systems both for the individual and for entire groups. In the realm of ideas the egalitarian gospel, the basis of all democratic orders, reinforces this trend by its demand for equal opportunities for all. This does not by any means imply that all differences between individuals are blurred, nor that there is no power differential in the present-day societies. On the contrary: with the incredible advance of the economy completely new positions of power, not comparable with anything in the past, have been created; that these have never had any immovable pre-ordained character is borne out by, if nothing else, the historical and social rise of the working class as a whole. The proletarian of 1850 has developed into a self-confident and fully equal member of society, who, with his trade unions, has built up positions of power of his own, on an equal footing with the old powers. The movement of fashion especially with its interplay of social etiquette and personal tact, uniformity and individual modification, creates distinctive features that sometimes help to underline very strongly the uniqueness of the individual.

Societies have indeed become far more fluid than they were in the past, as is revealed by innumerable present-day manifestations. One of the most important ones is the development of urban civilization, in which the blurring of all ranks has probably gone farthest as the populations of the large cities have increased. In this new environment vast numbers of people see all novelties almost from the first day of their appearance in public, so that the 'signal period' required by a new fashion to be accepted has been drastically reduced. This in turn is supported by an invention whose significance for fashion and its spread goes usually unrecognized: the ubiquitous electric light, which in the street as well as in theatre, concert, and festival halls regularly brings people into visual contact, enabling them to scrutinize the new fashions in the greatest detail.

The importance of artificial light in modern life was realized during the last war and sometimes even during its aftermath when public lighting had to be dimmed or completely blacked out. This had been, after all, the normal state of affairs in the towns at night before the invention of gaslight. At the same time the events for which large crowds congregate in the relative leisure of the evening, not only on festive, but also on a large number of other occasions (a stroll along the High Street to do a little window shopping, a visit to the cinema, or a meal out), are becoming more and more numerous since with the reduction of working hours the various leisure occupations have acquired far greater importance than ever before. Nor are the leisure hours necessarily spent in the home any longer, since rapid and cheap transport conveys people in comfort from the periphery of the cities to the centre of entertainment; there they will again have a chance to see the fashions, which they are able to buy since both the general standard of living of the great masses has risen, and mass production has made fashion articles cheaper. The effect of all these factors is becoming progressively stronger because not only the lower middle class, above all the various groups of white collar workers, but also the manual workers have acquired self-confidence and self-respect to the extent that they claim a fashionable style of life as their due. A certain resistance on the part of the old middle class, which quite naturally sees itself deprived of its former leading position and therefore reacts with some bitterness and resentment against the fashion-oriented behaviour of the great masses, is becoming increasingly evident; this is a topic which has almost become a hoary perennial of a certain type of social criticism.

Added to this communication by visual contact are now a sophisticated press, the colour supplements, magazines, and journals, all of which devote a great deal of space to fashion, quite apart from the extremely widely read, specialized fashion journals; the new mass media from film to television enable everyone to obtain additional information; even the general system of education may reinforce the trend. This effect of the urban environment is, however, by no means confined to city dwellers or to metropolitans; in fact, all the large cities are exposed to the glare of publicity, so that they radiate a fascinating glow to the rest of the population. All this is in turn most closely connected with the development of the economy; we are here faced with a very strange social system, in which the social spread of fashion, too, must assume new forms.

The fact that the leadership function of certain upper classes or estates has become considerably weaker compared with the past is alone sufficient to create a situation in which the stimuli for triggering off competition in fashion must be looked for in completely different quarters – as we shall see, in many quarters at the same time. This has certain consequences which are of decisive importance for fashion today and on which we must therefore focus our attention. Whereas in the past leadership in fashion was a more or less clear-cut issue, this is no longer the case; far from it. There thus enters a strong moment of uncertainty into the creation of fashion, which favours not only experimenting but also speculation. Since the consumer, too, has been sucked into the vortex of general social mobility, he becomes uncertain in his decisions, and all too often completely disoriented. This in turn has the effect of further accelerating the fashion change, and also of producing exaggerations that strike the moderate observer as distinctly comical as soon as they appear (for instance the Shimmy fashion after the first, and the 'swing-boy' after the second World War). One can say quite generally that this uncertainty, but also the readiness for rapid and frequent changes, must be most marked in those circles that are the most mobile. This has always applied to an extraordinary degree to certain groups of society, and fashion therefore produced particularly fantastic flowers among them at an early stage: we only have to remember the age of the intinerants and mercenaries. We meet a similar situation today in which we find the greatest quaintness, which all too often is no more than mere caprice, among the most mobile parts of the population, which generally include, for instance, the younger age groups. This attitude naturally finds its most extreme expression in the large cities. Women, especially the young ones, are more mobile than men; recently, however, the young men, too, have become active in the field of fashion; we shall discuss this phenomenon presently.

Apart from the fact that all the driving forces of fashion we have already mentioned continue to be effective, we have today, as an additional stimulus, the appearance of certain commanding public figures and certain activities that exert a fascinating attraction on the general public. The prototype of such commanding figures in the limelight was, for instance, King Edward VII (1841–1910) when he was Prince of Wales. These persons are surrounded by a certain nimbus, which most paradoxically is composed of a kind of fellow-feeling at a distance and the mysterious aura radiated across it. Basically it is the same nimbus that we find with actors, especially film stars, sports idols, and similar figures, who correspondingly exert the strongest possible influence on fashion: the public tries by every conceivable means to unearth the secret of their prestige. The simplest means of achieving this, and one that offers the user a kind of distinction into the bargain, is fashion. A young girl in the twenties adopting the hair-style worn by Greta Garbo consciously or subconsciously succumbed to the illusion that she radiated the same attraction as her idol. In the fifties, Brigitte Bardot exerted a similar influence. This applies equally to the most insignificant items of everyday use: when, for instance, an actress with an outstandingly beautiful complexion states that she uses a certain brand of soap or a special beauty aid she creates a stimulus of strong fashion currents for the same reason. Advertising of all kinds makes abundant use of this device.

In addition, however, it is characteristic of our own age that we choose our examples by no means only from circles of relatively remote and 'highly placed' persons, but are quite ready to pounce whenever we are offered something new. Accordingly items have become the fashion that have grown from the simplest everyday environment: such as the jersey or the track suit of the athlete, the shirt with collar attached and without tie of the manual worker (it has even become a permanent part of our wardrobe), the overall, the blue jeans or the farmer's breeches. Some items of clothing of this kind may even have been worn among certain circles for a long time before they became fashionable, such as the lumberjack's jersey (known for more than a hundred years) and the bush shirt. The blue jeans have been a characteristic feature of the American West since 1850; a single firm, 'Levi Strauss', were at first the leading manufacturers; hence the advertising slogan: 'The West grew up in Levis'.

The world-wide fashion of the blue jeans in the 1970s justifies a brief appreciation of their designer Levi Strauss, a young Bavarian Jew who emigrated to the American West in search of a fortune. He arrived with a roll of canvas as his only possession, which he wanted to sell to a tent maker. But when he realized that the miners in California needed above all stout trousers, he set up in the trouser business, opening his first shop in Sacramento. In 1853 we find him already in San Francisco, together with two of his brothers as partners; he moved several times to expand his business, opening a large store in Battery Street in 1870, which was destroyed during the earthquake and fire in 1906. The form of the blue jeans remained unchanged throughout this period, except that the original canvas gave way to blue twill. Strauss then introduced the copper rivets to reinforce the seams, and had them patented. Since 1930 women and girls, too, began to wear jeans, which today are perhaps the only universal item of clothing worn by the richest and the poorest alike. Although various new designs were introduced during their 120 years of existence, the blue version has successfully maintained its dominant position until today. Levi Strauss died a bachelor in 1902, leaving his business to his nephews, whose families are still running the firm.

Another feature characteristic of the present is the fact that occasionally entire folk costumes or parts of folk costumes of the lower classes are borrowed and used as fashion ideas (such as the Bavarian dirndl dress and the Basque beret). This also includes the exoticism of fashion, which has become an increasingly prominent factor since the end of the nineteenth century, although it was originally considered an abomination. In all these cases the influences which determine the unpredictable whims of fashion are usually very superficial; or a group that wears these items has moved for some reason or other into the limelight of publicity (the Korea jacket after the outbreak of the Korean war, the Indo-China line, with which the trouser suit is associated, during the Vietnam war, followed by the even more politically oriented Mao Look and the Che Guevara line come to mind). Since vast numbers of people are constantly on the lookout for and living in expectation of something new, the slightest impulse will sometimes be enough to induce a change of attitude. To this we must add the special groups we call pioneers of fashion; they are characteristic in that they do not mind even incurring ridicule so long as they can parade something new or bizarre in front of their amazed or puzzled public, as a model displays the latest creations at a fashion show. We must stress once again that here, too, there is evidence of uncertainty. The distinction from the rest now serves the self-assertion of the personality. It is therefore no surprise that we often find among these 'pioneers' certain youthful groups, such as, most recently, the denizens of the Left Bank – or the *Halbstarken*, *quaglioni*, beatniks, provos, *blousons noirs*, *gammler*, hippies.

This phenomenon as well as a mass of other observations we should have to mention here casts severe doubts on the validity of a principle that was widely discussed in Britain during and after the last war. This is the so-called 'utility' principle according to which functionalism as such could become creative or at least a contributory factor in the field of fashion. Our few remarks on the origin of dress have already demonstrated the small part usefulness played in it; and all further considerations showed that the irrational driving forces are strongly dominant in fashion. Many features praised as particularly practical when they were fashionable appear to us today to have been the height of inconvenience. What must be regarded as practical also depends on the continuously changing views of the people. Thus the British quickly got rid of their utility fashion as soon as they could with the gradual dismantling of the economic restrictions imposed by the war; the so-called 'reform-clothes' of the beginning of the century seem to add just another to the many ugly fashions we had to endure. Even the new style of art calling itself 'New Functionalism' is only a matter of fashion, like the contorted ornaments of Art Nouveau which today are enjoying a revival.

More significant than these considerations appears to be a distinct change in eroticism today, which favours particularly woman's need for distinction. Since the mutual attraction between the sexes is generally no longer regarded as something damnable, but as the most natural thing in the world, this factor must acquire great importance in the creation of fashion as a whole as well as for its variety. Whether as a wife or as a career woman, the modern woman wants to appear always attractive and always different; fashion becomes an immensely strong ally, which enables her to change her appearance and figure year in, year out. Since during the 'process of civilization' eroticism has furthermore been generally tamed, woman can and may yield to the appeal of eroticism with far less inhibition than ever before in history. For the game of the sexes has been severed from its purely sexual root and associated with aesthetics, so that erotic attraction no longer presents an immediate danger. From this aspect, too, the characteristic fashion-oriented behaviour of woman induces a speeding-up of the progress of fashion, and it does so in the brightest glare of publicity. This is the only explanation why the working woman has consistently rejected the wearing of standardized working clothes; even at work she wants to be accepted as a woman rather than as a neutral figure. To achieve this end she makes use of all the means at her disposal, above all of make-up, which in the cosmetics business has created one of the world's most powerful industries. Here, too, what in the past was the privilege of a few wealthy women has today become an everyday necessity of all women. But since every attraction is based on an ornament or decoration, this creates a strong impulse towards the general aesthetic design of our daily lives, which many other features have adversely affected to such an extent that we can well do with a little beauty in the more trivial aspects of life.

Obviously this has led to an enormous expansion of cosmetics, whose vital roots we have already uncovered. It has become not only fashion's most powerful ally, but an essential means of social equalization. Just as we find in animal life strong dislike of and indeed aggression against an individual whose appearance for some reason or other deviates from the accepted standard, something similar happens in human society. We need not think of the extreme case of albinism; it is enough to remember the consequences of having red hair to appreciate the importance of the role the outward appearance of a person plays in the process of social integration, which has the logical result of planned interference with his or her appearance. It has thus been pointed out that by disfiguring his appearance a person becomes isolated and communication with his environment is blocked. In view of the fact that in the advanced industrial societies not only objective (functional), but also extra-functional (e.g. social) skills are expected, the therapy of human disfigurement must steadily increase in importance, expanding into, among other fields, the scientific development of pharmacological treatment of the human appearance. This frees cosmetics from the role of merely routine and traditional aid; it becomes 'pheniatrics', as it has been called, which helps to cure 'phenomorbosity', that is, disfigurement and its various social consequences by means of 'pheniatric' aids, i.e. body care. In our view the term 'rehabilitation' used by Hans Freytag in this context is no exaggeration. But the real problem today is that cosmetics have become a reality for the great masses; men increasingly make use of them, whereas initially they were mainly the women's preserve.

It is perhaps also symptomatic that cosmetic surgery is today increasingly considered by health services and health insurance schemes as necessary as psychiatric and psychotherapeutic treatment. It has become accepted that a person's outward appearance can become a strong handicap, manifesting itself not only in a lack of communication, but ultimately even in an impairment of his entire social existence, i.e. in real infirmity. The development of the cosmetics industry thus proves, contrary to the claims of our professional social critics, a means not of 'manipulating', but of liberating man, now readily available to everybody instead of to a small privileged class. Recently W. E. J. Schneidrzik pointed out in this context that people asking for cosmetic surgery frequently suffer from severe neuroses. It has also been found that many prisoners sentenced to penal servitude are physically disfigured and corrective surgery often lowers the quota of recidivism. Disfigurement is therefore the cause of a genuine 'organic neurosis' (H. Meng).

Research into social prejudice of all kinds and the discrimination it causes against individuals and entire groups has revealed the importance of even trivial features of outward appearance as triggering factors. For it is only a small step from the rejection of someone because of a bad complexion to discrimination because of the colour of his skin. Although it will not be possible to standardize everybody's colour of skin, we should ponder about how strongly a person's entire social life can be impaired by his outward appearance.

21 The Spread of Fashion in Today's Society

Only when these conditions are understood can the way in which fashion spreads through society today be grasped. It accepts stimuli from all sides at once. Accordingly it becomes more and more difficult to trace the origin of even a single fashion in any detail; for the number of imponderables can occasionally become overwhelming. We can, however, produce a few fundamental yardsticks which can be discussed now we are about to come to the end of our considerations.

To begin with, women of all income groups (except typical country women) respond to fashion innovations great and small. In addition the younger age groups from about twenty to thirty years are more readily affected than the older groups. In their youth members of the older groups, too, were responsive to fashion, but their formerly changeable attitude froze, at a certain point in time, into a permanent attitude, a habit. We cannot therefore strictly claim that they are in no way affected by fashion, they have merely become 'bogged down' in the fashions of yesterday or the day before, have developed fixed habits and are therefore prepared to change their attitude in minor details only and to follow the development of fashion in small, cautious steps and at a distance. If we divide a given population into three age groups (twenty to thirty, thirty to fifty, and above fifty) and test their attitudes towards any article of fashion we shall clearly see that today's fashion is alive in the first age group, yesterday's in the second, and

19. Trouser suit by Courréges (1964). A creation that initiated the new version of the long line. *Courréges*

20. A simple version of the bikini (1971). *Camera Press*

the day before yesterday's in the third. Naturally this does not imply that the older groups have become completely unresponsive to fashion; they merely accept it more slowly than the others, in much smaller numbers, and in fewer respects, since in many of them the consumer habits have already become definitely fixed. We therefore see, as we investigate the spread of fashion, that it is the younger generation, its women and above all the young girls who are the first to adopt the new features. They are followed by a lower percentage of the next age group and, after a fair interval, by the oldest group with usually a very small involvement.

But there are other laws according to which fashion spreads; we must consider the economic position of the population and its division into urban and rural sectors in association with the previously described characteristics. It is extremely revealing in this respect to find that today wealth is no longer the sole criterion of susceptibility to fashion. Indeed, here a fundamental change has taken place from the situation in the nineteenth century; we have also seen that, unlike the old estates and aristocracies, 'the rich' no longer constitute a well-defined group. At the beginning of the nineteenth century the leaders of the new industrial society could, in the exuberance of their newly achieved political, economic, and social position, still cherish the illusion that within the general structure of society they had moved into the place previously occupied by the aristocracy of the Ancien Régime. But the subsequent development destroyed this illusion very thoroughly, which of course does not prevent certain members of this category from behaving even today as if they formed such an aristocracy. They include a number of exotic dukes and princes who because of the backwardness of their countries can afford such an attitude even now. But they are a tiny minority, out of all proportion to the publicity accorded to them by certain illustrated weeklies writing at great length and detail of their so-called achievements and deeds. Basically they belatedly play the same part as

Russian grand dukes a hundred years ago, who night after night gambled fortunes away at Baden-Baden and Monte Carlo. They are conspicuous, certainly; but their significance in fashion, let alone in any other field, is negligible. There remain a few personalities who radiate a genuine fashion-creating prestige because of their eminent position; but these personalities, too, have become rare among the top circles of the well-to-do. As a dethroned oriental potentate remarked, the day may not be far away when only the King of England will enjoy such prestige, provided he still has the means that classify him as a member of the top class of the rich.

A radical change has indeed taken place here: only some of the very rich are active as leaders in fashion; this function has quite definitely passed to the medium-high and middle income groups, which are also much more significant economically. This can be clearly seen in the development of the motorcar: the extremely expensive Rolls-Royce has outwardly remained almost unchanged for decades; the mass-produced cars of the medium price range, on the other hand, are strongly affected by the trends of fashion. One might even hazard the statement that the very rich display a tendency to inconspicuousness which, among men as well as women, results in a distinct conservatism as far as fashion is concerned. There may be a desire to hide from the great public. The middle income groups, in contrast, are particularly responsive to fashion today, and it must be emphasized that among women this mobility reaches down to the lowest income groups: a single glance at the shopping centres of the big cities after the shops are closed will confirm this. There the new fashions are taken up, usually very soon after they have appeared, by the female personnel of the large stores, who are economically very weak indeed. Today it is therefore no longer correct to say that the new fashions slowly percolate from the top income groups down to ever-widening circles of society. In fact they begin among the middle groups (with the upper middle groups possibly taking a certain lead), from where they spread simultaneously upwards and downwards, with the lower income groups of the younger section of the female population showing a considerably higher mobility and adaptability than their equivalents of the highest income groups.

Finally, the total environment, above all the big city, also favours the development of fashion. City dwellers are generally avid for anything that is new on the scene; their attitude to fashion is no exception. We thus find regularly today that the fashion spreads from the metropolis first to large cities, then to medium-sized and ultimately to small towns and rural areas (in so far as the latter accept fashion ideas at all in time and not after such long delay that it is no longer regarded as a fashion). Certain of the large cities and capitals such as Paris have taken over the role of leadership in fashion in the most unmistakable manner. We should like to point out that the leading role of Paris is not based on any special spirit of progressiveness, of receptiveness to current ideas. The rhythm of life in France is really different. In fact, that surviving spirit of the aristocracy and the feudalist bourgeoisie so significant for the beginning of the nineteenth century is still very much alive in France. The representatives of the Paris Haute Couture thus still behave all too often as feudal potentates of fashion, and this will naturally never fail to make a deep impression on certain circles. On the other hand the prestige of Paris is, after all, extremely durable, so that it has been able to persist without much opposition even after other centres such as Vienna, Rome, and New York had been active in the realm of fashion for various lengths of time. It is a prestige that can be traced back as far as the age of Louis XIV; added to this is the fact that in the course of time countless industries ancillary to fashion have concentrated in Paris and gradually acquired an almost institutional power of persistence.

But in spite of an overwhelming acceleration of fashion development, it happens over and over again that implements that had been fashion crazes suddenly become permanently established; to name only three examples: the Oxford shoe, the wristwatch, and the fountain pen, which after the second World War was replaced by the ball pen. As consumer goods they belong to the essential inventory of our everyday life; fashion thus no longer modifies use as such, but only the form of presentation. The same applies to countless trivial items, such as crossword puzzles, astrology and horoscopes; ping pong endures, whereas yo-yo was quickly forgotten and is perhaps quite unknown to the younger generation today. Expensive consumer goods, too, may start as a fashion, gradually to become part of the modern comforts, without which we can no longer imagine life: the motorcar, the washing machine and the refrigerator.

Beyond these problems we merely have to consider the graph of the social spread of fashion; here a few important points which are able to complete the picture of fashion in the modern world will become evident. At the beginning of a new fashion development we regularly note a distinct hesitation; this period can vary in length: one wants to keep in step with the fashion without being ahead of it. The pioneers are thus always left on their own, if only for a few weeks. After this period of hesitation the wave of fashion spread invariably rises, reaching its crest at increasing speed, only to subside rapidly afterwards. This is the normal picture of development. But just as the origin of a fashion is often due to quite accidental external influences, this progression may be abruptly and prematurely ended for reasons quite as accidental. This includes not only typical abortive fashions and speculative failures that are simply not accepted by the public, but also quite unpredictable external events such as a sudden break in the weather at the end of the summer, or a war. The subject of prematurely passing fashions has, incidentally, received scant attention so far by workers in this field, the most important exception being the American Paul Nyström. From the economic aspect there are several ways out: a switchover from city to rural consumers perhaps, or to another continent where the summer is only beginning. But there is another possibility: a fashion may survive a bad season, and at the beginning of the next identical season immediately catch on with full force; during the first fine summer's day suddenly all the women without exception appear in the same rig. This is a case of a latent fashion effect, which raises the searching question whether this can be recognized beforehand to enable the industry to plan accordingly. One symptom at any rate is worth mentioning: if shortly before the beginning of autumn light summer fabrics or at the end of winter furs are still being bought one can expect that the same patterns and models will still be bought and worn at the beginning of the next corresponding season – unless other unforeseeable events intervene.

The previously mentioned Paul Nyström drew a very important distinction here, which to us seems to be significant for the understanding of the social spread of fashion. For the graph of the consumer purchase of an article of fashion and that of its effective use are not the same: a fashion is always worn for a longer period than it is bought. If, then, it is still bought at the end of a season one can safely predict that it will still be worn later. At the beginning of a fashion, sales and use increase at exactly the same rate; at the crest sales mostly drop abruptly, whereas use decreases much more slowly. This persistence of use is quite simply determined by the need to 'wear out' the articles. Conversely the producers must ensure that particularly conspicuous fashion items are not made of too durable material, so that the path of the following fashion is smoothed by rapid wear and tear. If the quality of the material were too high, the old fashion would become an obstacle to the development of the new. This problem has often been misunderstood in the past so that there was a tendency to deduce a general inferiority of the quality of fashionable consumer goods. Certainly the durability of fabrics, especially of ladies' wear, which are subject to rapid changes of fashion, is less than that of, for instance, men's materials. But since fashion competition has recently become so extraordinarily keen, quality has had to move from durability to, for example, the colours, the printing, and the originality of the pattern, to which accordingly a great amount of thought, experimenting, and the invention of completely new methods of improvement and refinements are devoted. In other items of the ladies' wardrobe less subject to changes in fashion, such as tailor-made dresses, the emphasis of quality is still on durability.

The graph of the social spread of fashion can, however, be analysed even more precisely in another respect. If we look at it from a purely static point of view, we shall learn something about the general trend only, not about the individuals making up the wave and about their behaviour. But this trend can assume a special form in at least one respect: there is no need at all for the effective followers of a fashion to observe its cycle from beginning to end. In fact we find quite a number of persons who abandon an existing fashion even before it has reached its climax. This is also associated with competition with and distinction from the others, and induces the avant-garde either to adopt an even newer fashion provided it already exists, or to experiment for the time being. At such periods we have a tendency for the so-called fads to occur, minor variants of fashion of sometimes extremely short life.

This behaviour is readily understood if one realizes the dramatic speed at which a fashion spreads at its climax, a speed which is, incidentally, not entirely due to outright purchases; an additional factor is that the avant-gardists often give away articles they had bought a few months previously to be ahead of the others. At the time of the sales standardization is the order of the day; but at the same time it triggers all the impulses which help to smooth the transition to the subsequent fashion. It is thus necessary for every fashion to 'outlive' itself, either

The Spread of Fashion in Today's Society 183

by becoming a standard feature of everyday life, or by lingering on for a while among the less affluent.

In this respect the changes that have taken place with the introduction of seasonal sales are very instructive. Whereas in the past these sales were mainly clearance sales to get rid of leftovers at considerably reduced prices, the situation today is completely different and no longer confined to items that have become old-fashioned. On the contrary, sales today have acquired a special importance in the spread of fashion in that they offer at the lowest possible prices goods specially produced and bought for the purpose; this definitely helps to popularize the new fashion. The average customer today strictly refuses to 'snap up' out-of-fashion articles, not even at give-away prices. This is further evidence that the great masses have needs to be satisfied, and that the fashion sales do precisely this. But since the sales are aimed directly at the great masses they bring boredom with the new fashion dangerously close. Whereas it was possible in the past to get rid of remnants in the provincial backwaters or in rural areas, this now applies only within the limitations of the already described conditions; illustrated weeklies and fashion journals, film and television spread the knowledge of new developments everywhere. This affects above all the young women and girls we have already mentioned. At best one can hope to sell the remnants to the older generation which in its attitude towards fashion regularly trails behind the younger generation.

Added to all the already discussed factors determining the social spread of fashion must be a number of others, some of which have a speeding-up, others a slowing-down effect on development; they may, for instance, be economic. Besides the general improvement of communications, publicity for fashion by many fashion journals, and the patterns, with their sales pushed by highly professional advertisers, the establishment of cheap mass consumer industries in all fields has had a decisive effect. These industries could, however, develop only after the invention of standardization of production, which resulted in the introduction of ready-to-wear clothing; this replaced the expensive bespoke tailoring and made fashion novelties available to ever-expanding sections of the population at reasonable prices. It is extremely significant to observe that today not only the Haute Couture, but also the better-class ready-to-wear establishments make use of the fashion show for publicity purposes. This provides evidence that fashion design does not necessarily lead to inferior products, but that modern ready-to-wear clothes have reached a standard of quality that must be seen (as is its purpose) to be believed. Whereas initially ready-to-wear was synonymous with cheap (for instance, working and workmen's clothes), influenced as it was to a certain extent by the mass production of police and army uniforms, this class of products has gradually improved in quality to its present standard of excellence.

This development is by no means at an end but is still continuously advancing. To appreciate this we need merely remember that there was initially no difference between right and left shoes, shoes being perhaps one of the first items of mass production as we know it. The customer had to break them in by walking in them. (In the East this is still the case.) We have only to compare this situation with today's range and variety to see the progress that has been made. Even surgical boots are today mass-produced by specialized firms. To this example can be added many others from the large number of everyday consumer goods.

22 Old Techniques Produce New Fashions

In its drive to develop its potentialities fashion affects not only man as a whole, but all technical means available so long as they produce particularly aesthetic effects. There are in addition the previously mentioned facilities of mass production, which basically affect not only the distinctive function of a colour, a pattern, a design, a texture, but also the possibilities of a social spread of fashion.

Since man first entered the scene he has therefore made far greater efforts in the invention of methods, techniques, and machinery for the manufacture and finishing of objects to adorn the body than for the satisfaction of immediate needs. But when man used fibres and hair to spin yarn as the raw material for fabrics and plait work the economic requirements were at first relatively small; so were the numbers of people involved. The situation did not change until the development of the advanced civilizations of antiquity, which comprised larger populations than ever before. Since then it has become more and more acute until the age of the popular democracies and mass production. The development of the silk industry in fact heralded the first great economic clash between China and the rest of the world. Since about the third century B.C. China enjoyed a clear monopoly position in silk, producing considerable quantities of silk cloth for the trade along the Silk Roads from East to West. Later on, between 1000 and 1200, sericulture spread to Byzantium and to Spain and Italy. Since the Middle

Ages we find rising production figures of silk cloth in Europe, ever subject to changes of fashion down to our own days. Silk could not be ousted by the man-made fibres, although since the end of the nineteenth century they have conquered the market with incredible speed and introduced fashion innovations of their own, of which the most outstanding is the nylon stocking.

In addition to spinning we soon find weaving; here, too, individual production in the home was initially the rule. But it is astonishing to note at how early a stage mechanical production started. The loom in various forms is very ancient indeed, and occurs in Egypt already around 2000 B.C. Naturally it was hand-operated at first, but at the beginning of the eighteenth century the mechanical loom was invented, and soon connected with the steam engine. It is interesting that it is precisely here that automatic control techniques for machines were first conceived; Jacquard's mechanical loom, for instance, was operated from about 1816 on a kind of punched-card system, which prepared the way for automation. This happened at a time when the types of fabric already differed extraordinarily, so that soon these machines were expected to meet the most stringent requirements. But we do not wish to repeat what can be read at greater detail in any book on the history of textiles; we only want to show how new fashions arise from old techniques, how through the change in the modern style of life long-familiar techniques are modified for completely new forms of application, thereby undergoing a considerable change in function.

We thus find that knitting joined the techniques of weaving in the thirteenth century; naturally, this, too, was at first a handicraft. But it produced a fabric which, as will be shown here, has again become popular, and on a worldwide scale at that, in our current fashion; what is more, within the concept of this fashion it has become the key product for innumerable designs for certain functions and activities. The technical equipment of the old weaving mill requires the threads to be under tension; the resulting fabrics have little elasticity. Since in knitting the connection of the threads differs basically from that in weaving in that they do not need to be taut, the fabrics produced are extremely elastic as well as porous. They cling to the body most effectively and also facilitate the breathing of the skin. The last point is so important to modern hygienists that the wearing of knitted fabrics has produced a minor revolution: Professor Jaeger's 'normal underwear' met with sensational success, which survives in today's porous underwear and has become an enduring feature of modern living. This underwear has become so completely accepted by European and American workers that after work and at home they walk about in their singlets only; they consider it quite respectable among the family and close friends; for a time it was to some extent even an occupational status symbol to distinguish manual workers from other classes of employee.

But much more important than the porousness of these fabrics is their ability plastically to reproduce the shape of the body. At the very moment when emphasis on natural shape, such as that of the female breasts, was connected with new aesthetic stimuli, this old technique of making fabrics naturally experienced another, glorious revival.

The first features that benefited from the new material were, however, not women's breasts, but men's calves. This decided the whole of the first period of development of knitwear fashions, whose existence has been proved beyond doubt from the thirteenth century onwards. A further factor was the invention of a knitting machine by William Lee in 1589, which long preceded that of machinery for other fabrics; several improvements were quickly introduced and the machine was amazingly efficient; it was responsible for the first worldwide spread of fashions in knitwear, whose functions, however, were dictated and curbed by the general line of the fashion of those days. The knitwear articles were not displayed in isolation, but usually in association with the general style of fashion, in the simplest form as stockings for men and women, then as golf-hose (with knee breeches) and finally as hose for men. This tended to emphasize the male genitals, worn conspicuously and magnified proudly in a special compartment, and the man's calves. These, too, must have had a kind of sexually ostentatious function; this is proved by the general use of false calves, with probably the same purpose as padded brassieres and falsies worn by young girls today. It is interesting to note that pantie-hose for women has, except for professional use by tennis players and ballerinas, acquired general importance only in our own days, when shorter skirts and particularly the mini-skirt have created an urgent demand for it.

After its first flowering as a men's fashion, however, the knitwear fashion sank into oblivion for a time, after the long trousers of the democratic industrial civilization had displaced the aristocratic knee breeches and reduced the role of the stocking and hose to the minor one of the sock. Even this was replaced by peasants and workers, and, for a longer period still, by soldiers with the so-called toe-rags (Prince Alberts). This is further evidence of the length of time the uniform of the modern male required for its development and the tortuous ways it took until it reached its present perfection. But from about 1870 onwards knitwear fashions suddenly received a fresh impulse which immediately expressed itself in very diverse forms and uses. This new revival was supported from the eighteen-sixties on by a new and more efficient machine, the knitting machine designed by Lamb. For the first time it became possible to produce a large number of new fashion designs almost simultaneously; they have ever since formed an important part of modern man's fashion inventory.

Apart from the various forms of porous underwear (differing in material and cut, and including the most delicate, gossamer-like luxury lingerie for women, little more than an extension of the skin), the use of knitwear now extends, with the development of popular sports taking place at the same time, to the completely new material of stockinette. The stockinette clothing of sportsmen has become an integral part of modern man's functional clothing since the 1880s. We are apt to forget this all too easily when we look at the old stockinette articles, whose patterns and designs appear grotesque to our taste; at best they linger on precariously (with or without stripes) as fancy dress items; the models developed for men and women have become more and more sophisticated and are subject to fashion trends of their own. These trends are of course usually influenced by the great sporting events, the Olympic Games for example, which today have the same signal function as the great festivities and triumphal processions of the past. There are also the creations and decisions by outstanding personalities in sports, such as the French tennis champion Suzanne Lenglen, who was the first to play in a short skirt without tights and thus made the bare leg acceptable in female sports. Bathing costumes, too, are part of sportswear; they were a completely new idea, for previously people went into the water either completely naked or fully clothed. This item of clothing developed rapidly from the most monstrous forms disfigured by frills and bloomers to one of the unique creations of our time, the bikini, as the ultimate expression of the two-part bathing costume. The prototype of the bikini was found in the mosaics of a Roman villa at Piazza Armerina (Sicily) dating from the turn of the third and fourth century A.D.; it particularly emphasizes the girl's abdomen. The bikini corresponds to a new form of erotico-aesthetic appreciation in which the sun-bronzed skin of the female body and its velvet sheen has attained an importance as never before. The male counterpart of the bikini are the light, neat briefs which have at long last replaced our grandfathers' triangular bathing trunks with something far more attractive, made possible only by the new material.

Nor is this all. Sports are almost synonymous with youth. The new fashions generally develop along a line that emphasizes youthfulness; this also requires that they should be relatively easy on the purse, a feature facilitated by mass production. This opened up completely new possibilities of fashion development in which knitwear fashion once again acquired prominence. It is most significant that it was no longer confined to accessories but assumed the character of a fashion leader in its own right. It is remarkable that the collections of these new garments immediately developed on a broad basis from the cheapest mass product to the genuine luxury model. This is a completely new trend in the way in which modern fashion spreads; for in the past such a process of differentiation began only after some garment had been accepted by the public for a considerable time.

All this applies particularly to the jumper, perhaps the most typical item of clothing of our time, worn by men and women alike. Since the end of the first World War it has spread to every country under the sun; at the end of the second World War it was given another boost in the basements of the Left Bank by Juliette Greco. Initially the jumper was the expression of an informal style of life which sought freedom of movement for the body and did not want to be hemmed in by narrow and restricting waistcoats or jackets made of heavy woven fabrics. It then became, as a female garment, the symbol of a new erotic sensitivity, in an unselfconscious fashion modelling the breasts as the visible secondary sex characteristic in woman's dress. This also resulted in a general change in women's posture. Unlike mediaeval posture which, also with erotic intent, pushed the abdomen strongly to the fore so that the shoulders drooped and the breasts became insignificant as a sexual attraction (they may have been altogether tucked away), that of young girls today keeps the abdomen well in and squares the shoulders, so that the breasts stand out conspicuously; they are further emphasized by brassieres and the jumper. In sleeveless dresses fitted in the waist the shoulders and exposed upper arms are prominent; their erotic function, like that of the breasts, is undeniable.

For the man the same garment has a different significance altogether: it serves mainly to lessen the formality of everyday life; it is accordingly worn not so much at work as during time-off. The jumper thus makes its decisive contribution to the democratization of modern society; there only remains the question how far it will be possible gradually to convert the renunciation by the male sex of fashion into a new form of life. For the time being a clear separation of the two worlds seems to be taken for granted by many. The professions thus continue to cling to the old puritan uniform with its bias against anything fashionable, which is considered trivial and frivolous. This only changes as soon as the men leave their work behind, in the evening, at weekends, on holiday and on journeys. A completely new world opens up to us, which has also created a new, nature-loving style adapted to outdoor life. It is significant that attempts are now made to launch a more imaginative style of men's jackets for just this purpose under the name of leisure wear. This new form of male dress partly represents a further development of sportswear. But gradually special clothing for sports and hunting has become clearly distinct from that now worn generally for spare-time pursuits. As leisure becomes more abundant for more and more people the chance increases that men, too, will enter a new phase of increased fashion activity. For the time being, however, they are still existing in a kind of schizophrenic situation in which the puritan still hiding in every man devotes his life to ceaseless work from Monday to Friday, but becomes a different person on Saturday and Sunday. This created, at the beginning of the century, the Anglo-Saxon weekend style, which to begin with expressed itself in a simple neglect of bourgeois gentility and found relaxation in a kind of well-ordered indolence. It remains to be seen whether, to what extent and for how long the relaxed attitude of leisure time can replace the hallowed custom of rigorous suppression of the temptations of fashion and achieve a revolution in the fashion of workaday clothes.

A new phase began for the technology of textile manufacture at the end of the nineteenth century with the explosive development of man-made fibres, which were increasingly added to animal and plant fibres. While in the metal industry the age of steel gave way to that of aluminium and plastics, a similar development took place in the textile industry involving a change from natural to synthetic fibres. Artificial silk (rayon) with its rather obtrusive sheen consisted of organic substances; its use was rather short-lived, and the material was soon replaced by various types of man-made (chemical) fibre, which are completely synthetic. These have revolutionized the old manufacturing techniques and made entirely new textures possible. At the same time existing dyeing methods were largely modified, not only because of the development of the chemistry of dyestuffs which went hand in hand with progress in all the other fields, but also because the combination of man-made fibres and the new dyes produced colourings that had never been possible before. The colour film with its colour mixtures deviating from the natural also had an influence that should not be underestimated. To sum up, new inventions have revolutionized old techniques and thereby unexpectedly created new impulses for creative fashion design.

21. Simple minidress (1971). *Camera Press*

22. Hot pants, London (1971). *Camera Press*

23 First Interlude: Topless or Not?

Topless dresses and bathing costumes suddenly appeared in many places in the early summer a few years ago. The press and other mass media were at once full of ironical, contemplative, angry, damning and social critical remarks, and a great German philosopher, who had never before lost his thread since he read everything from notes (out of fear of misunderstanding himself) suddenly left the rostrum without a word when a few girl students danced around him in topless dresses. Women and young girls, however, seem to have a lively interest in this fashion: California has night clubs with 'topless' hostesses; you can see them also in the Playboy Clubs in many American cities; in Mediterranean summer resorts you can admire young women in evening gowns that cover their bare breasts only with a transparent veil. Rumour also has it that in West Germany the police, after a complaint, inspected two ladies that had turned up in a night club in topless evening gowns; strangely enough they found no grounds for action. The subject was also taken up among the highest government circles. The pronouncement was rather matter-of-fact: fears were voiced that the fashion would not be just worn by the 'right' women, young ones that really had something to offer in topless dresses. Thus one controversy followed another. In view of this situation we may be permitted to make a few observations that can contribute to an interpretation and therefore a 'defusing' of this problem.

The question whether topless or not is obviously generally associated with the plunging neckline. We also know that this is nothing new. During the Renaissance even burgher's wives in German cities wore boldly plunging necklines. It was said at the time that the ladies 'opened the shutters'. In Burgundy women had even appeared completely in the nude on certain festive occasions, or wore only veils that were totally transparent: transparent too was the chemise, fashionable during the Directorate in France (1795–9) under the *Reine du Directoire*, Madame de Récamier. The see-through-shift had a high waist, so that the breasts protruded beyond the loose edge of the material. Although this aspect was often welcome, there were exceptions, because the neckline was sometimes particularly revealing on those wearers who could least afford it. This provoked a criticism that was not moral, but aesthetic. One may also be allowed to quote an observation by Talleyrand, who during a ball felt embarrassed by the appearance of an amply endowed lady with an unusually plunging neckline. His partner in conversation asked him: 'Have you ever seen anything like this?' 'Not since I was weaned' was Talleyrand's reply. But such revealing features occur also in folk costumes, for instance in the bodice worn in Alpine regions: the breasts are presented to the beholder as in a 'basket'.

Quite apart from these phenomena we are, however, tempted to think that today's topless fashion has a special aspect that has not yet been discussed. We occasionally find another type of topless fashion that had no connection with the plunging neckline in that it revealed the breasts not only as a result of a general display of the woman's neck, back, and shoulders, but quite independently from the neckline, in their own right as it were. A picture exists of Agnes Sorel, mistress of King Charles VII of France from 1442 to 1450, who loved to appear with bare breasts at minor receptions; many (probably very flat-chested) court ladies objected to this. We have other pictures and reports of this kind, so that a long history can perhaps be claimed for this aspect of fashion, too. A few years ago we ourselves raised the question whether in the course of women's emancipation young ladies would soon regard it as their right to appear 'topless' on certain occasions.

This brings us to the crux of the problem. We think that the topless fashion, recently so suddenly erupted on both sides of the Atlantic, is strictly confined to a certain young age group of women who generally occupy a pioneering position in present-day fashion development. This is very much in contrast with the past, when fashion innovations were presented mostly by the women of the middle and older age groups. Today, however, the young women belong to a movement of their own which made them attempt publicly to burn their brassieres. And, if the topless fashion is confined to them, even the fussiest aesthetes may rest content.

It can be predicted with the same certainty that this fashion will be limited to certain occasions, such as, without doubt, sunbathing on the beach. We can also imagine that in future less restrictive clothes will be preferred for certain types of sport. Something similar applies to evening wear for major and minor occasions. This immediately raises a further question, that of make-up. Talk about making up and powdering the breasts for topless wear seems merely a logical extension of existing habits. The careful treatment of the face simply includes shoulders and breasts. Already in the mid-fifties an almost topless evening dress was seen in the collection of a prominent couturier in Madrid. Since it was worn by a model of hardly eighteen, even the most fastidious observer would have been hard pressed to find it objectionable. We have emphasized on various occasions that young women react quite differently from men when their bodies are revealed, although some men already tend to adopt the valuations characteristic of the female frame of mind. What could so often be misunderstood as a purely erotic temptation is in reality no more than an expression of the new position of woman in society, especially the presentation of her own body, which with increasing independence also acquires a 'public' significance. This attitude of women will perhaps spread from the primarily involved young men to men as a whole. We can very well imagine, for instance, that only the older generation of men objects to this fashion, seeing in it sexual revelation, whereas the young men will very rapidly take it in their stride.

The final point to be discussed is whether this fashion will last. In view of the frequent recurrence of plunging necklines and topless fashions reaching back as far as the Cretan-Minoic and Egyptian civilizations around 2000 B.C., but in view also of its repeated disappearance, one could assume that this time, too, it might only be short-lived. It is at any rate remarkable that this fashion is adopted today not just by a tiny minority, but by large numbers although it is certain that it will remain confined to young women and to certain occasions. We should moreover like to reject a valuation of the whole phenomenon in terms of strong erotic overtones and emphasize instead its significance as an expression of woman's emancipation.

The woman's outline as a whole has nevertheless erotic importance in every era. We only have to remember that since the beginning of the twenties skirts have become shorter and shorter and the appearance of woman has drastically changed. The slim line, in which the natural curves of the body are clearly revealed, a general elongation of the outline, above all a slimming of the thighs caused by a regular pursuit of sports that has put an end to the 'short-legged look', and finally a permanent tan acquired through increased outdoor life in fresh air, sun and water and having the effect of natural make-up (above all rouge): all these factors have combined to change the erotic aspect of woman completely from anything we have ever seen before. When we look at the many nations on earth in the present and the past, as well as at our own history we shall readily appreciate that the differences between what various people or groups consider an erotic temptation are extraordinary. It has above all become evident that the execration of the naked body as an invention of the devil is only the warped notion of a small sect of religious maniacs, whose influence is confined to a minority of the so-called 'western' world (including the puritan and exaggeratedly prudish socialist cultures); because it was economically very powerful, it was possible for a time to mistake it for 'the world' as a whole. But this world, too, has for the last fifty years been in the throes of a fundamental change of all social and therefore also all erotic relations. It can then be safe to assume that the climate of experimentation of the most recent times will also affect the immediate future, until the new vision of woman has become an element of style in its own right. Only then will fashion become stabilized again. But we are certain that in these fashions of the future emancipated woman in the popular democracies will again and again return to a display of the naked breast as a symbol of the achievement of freedom in her everyday life. But even then this revelation will always be restricted to special occasions.

24 Second Interlude: Fashion and Anti-Fashion

The question raised by the title of this chapter lacks precision, because the origin of the new fashion itself lacks precision. Juliette Greco grew up in the basements of the Left Bank where immediately after the war not only was an antimorality evolved in opposition to the official morality of the bourgeois world, but also an anti-fashion. Boussac, the powerful industrial tycoon from Lyons, tried by launching Christian Dior to build up the French fashion export industries, and, with a neo-romantic fashion called the New Look, to make us forget the horrors of the war.

But the reaction of the young generation to the war was totally different. Although with the hindsight of the seventies we know that it ultimately started a new youth fashion, the original motive was anti-fashion. Juliette Greco's black jumper expressed political protest, it radiated black humour and the negative philosophy of Jean-Paul Sartre, it was also intimately related to the later ostentatious slovenliness of the beatniks of Greenwich Village and the hippies of San Francisco. Today Juliette probably no longer wears a black jumper even at weekends, but has become a steady customer of the great Paris fashion houses. But the trend she started long ago in the gloom of the rat-infested basements has developed and expanded into a new use of fashion by which youth protests against the world of the bourgeoisie and of affluence. That it is possible to trace the development of a new fashion rhythm suggests that

Second Interlude: Fashion and Anti-fashion 199

youth's fashion protest will last longer than many a naïve observer might assume. It is not a short-term whim of fashion, forgotten within a few years, but a new departure from which many future individual fashions will evolve.

The anti-fashion trend of youth manifested itself already at the beginning of the century and is a process that has repeated itself in various guises to our own days and assumes ever new forms. It combines with a new *weltanschauung* which adds an anti-ideology to anti-fashion. The beatniks protested with their straggly beards against the public smugness of the clean shave which suppresses the animal growth of hair in the man's face. The hippies wear their hair long in protest against the crew cut, and prefer 'Mother Nature' to bourgeois conventions. They are all opposed to elegance and the unimaginative correctness of the white-collar workers and the executives in their spotless white shirts, artistically knotted ties, complete with pearl tiepin. But the aseptic, brightly lit atmosphere of the office does not allow for the dark side of life. The beat generation said a clear, loud 'No' to all this. At first in gentle, lyrical, unconventional poems, occasionally in cries of despair, and finally in student and youth revolts or in the spontaneous appearance of loafers of all kinds, different wherever in the world they are found but united in the same protest against middle-class morality. This gives them a unique outlook on the world, which in certain conditions is confined to the few moments of a 'happening' or expresses itself in a rapid succession of fashion currents in the visual arts, from pop art to op art, pretending to be anti-art. They influence even the great fashion magazines. The pioneer magazine *Rags* has taken the place of *Vogue* and *Harper's Bazaar*; it has set itself the task of breaking the tradition, above all of putting an end to the cheap gloss of the always somewhat gushing fashion reportages: 'Fashion is not fashionable any more.' That something new is being born can easily be seen on Telegraph Avenue in Berkeley,

California, the Fifth Avenue of anti-civilization, and in London's Carnaby Street and King's Road.

But the outcome of this anti-fashion is by no means the extinction of fashion, it is merely the beginning of a new dimension which lends concrete expression to the life-spirit of modern youth. Its creative force acts on ever new starting points, for instance the Beatles and the beat music of recent times, whose disruptive effect can be compared only with the metaphysical depth of jazz in the twenties. We say 'disruptive', because the effect of these eruptions is the amalgamation and break-up of the social class problems of the nineteenth century and their replacement with new principles of social stratification, to which the polarization of young and old is of greater importance than the former confrontation of proletariat and bourgeoisie. But it would be a profound mistake to assume that this is the beginning of a rejection of fashion. Shakespeare already lets his stage servants – the servants and fools of Shakespeare's plays are the sixteenth-century beatniks and the underground of old London – discuss the problem: fashion not only makes the ordinary man giddy, it ultimately affects even the behaviour of the critic and makes him its follower against his will.

This alters the problem radically, especially if we consider the earlier approach to the question of youth fashion, which is, after all, basically nothing new. In contrast we are today confronted with a structural change, since in modern societies youth plays a much greater role than ever before. We are not concerned with the fact that a youth fashion exists, but that the youth fashions will determine fashion as a whole because of the structurally changed position of youth in modern society. On the basis of this change one can predict an influence of youth fashion on adult fashions.

But this observation is not enough to shed light on the meaning of this change. For young women began to play a prominent role in fashion as early as the middle of last century.

Whereas the young women of that period displayed great determination to take advantage of all the tricks of fashion, the men, even the young ones, remained largely in the background. One could go so far as to claim that, following the trend which has become more and more conspicuous since the reformation and with which we are already familar, they deliberately refrained from any fashion-oriented activity. This self-inflicted asceticism characterized the bourgeois era for centuries. Except during the period of Romanticism men played practically no part on the stage of fashion throughout the nineteenth century. This state of affairs ended only with the first World War, although it must be pointed out that as early as the beginning of the twentieth century youth movements appeared on the scene which, exactly like some of today's movements, took up the position of anti-fashion. But in those days this was merely a fringe phenomenon. The basic situation for young men was that they shared the typical male prejudice, stemming from the great renunciation of fashion during the puritanical industrial revolution, against a too fashion-oriented treatment of outward appearance. Symptomatic of this is the dull grey suit, whose line remained almost completely static, without any major changes.

A minor change in adult fashions became, however, noticeable between 1920 and 1930; but during this period youth was relatively inactive. This was the situation in those days: the same people who were old on the eve of the 1914 war had become considerably more youthful ten years later. Pictures and photographs of this period readily confirm a remarkable change in the life of the thirty to fifty year group. On the sidelines the various youth movements remained relatively ineffectual; at most they developed an anti-fashion as a protest against the bourgeois type of uniformity both in Europe and in America.

We thus find a fashion movement among American college students which has been going on for the last fifty years or so, but which is typical in that it represents only a brief phase in a man's life. In contrast with the well-groomed appearance of the smart businessman the young students, male and female, began to dress in a deliberately sloppy fashion. The university campus was a world of its own, in which dressing sportily and casually was preferred to the observance of 'the thing to do'. It was natural that this world should, to begin with, remain a world apart. In addition, those it affected suddenly changed their behaviour as soon as they left college. Seen within the context of life as a whole, this special fashion was transient, covering the episode of adolescence. It reached its end with the initiation of the individual into adult life.

Something else has happened in recent times which without doubt has the same roots, but deflects the movement into a different direction. Youth has become creative in the field of fashion not only as a special group but in its totality. For the first time a new element is projected into the foreground, the influence of youth on fashion as such. This manifests itself in two ways: in the first instance, it obviously determines the fashions of youth. But it is much more important that the enormous significance of these youthful fashions is slowly beginning to change the fashions of older people too. This structural change appears to be all the more lasting in that parallel with it runs a change of consciousness; there is a rising awareness of the uniqueness of this new situation, which also develops a new attitude to fashion, new yardsticks of valuation, new guiding ideas, a new outlook on the world, becoming more and more widespread not only politically but also aesthetically and in the realm of fashion. A far-reaching and very broadly-based youth revolution which is about to change the whole of society is unfolding before our eyes.

This influence, incidentally, is the only way that remains to youth to preserve itself beyond its own limits. For youth is a state that quickly passes. A slogan advises us: 'Don't believe anybody over thirty.' Well, we soon pass the age of thirty, and thereafter are inexorably absorbed by the adult world. But this world, too, will change because those who enter it now have been through the comprehensive process of modern youth's growing self-awareness, which will have transformed them.

This is a state which has been found to exist in no other society known to us so far. One could almost say that before our time youth never existed as a large group with an awareness of its own. This is easily explained. If one turns up the old Prussian statistics and consults the tables about the working population, the period of full-time employment extended from fourteen to fifty-five. But at fourteen a person has only just left his childhood behind and enters adolescence. If at the same time he begins his working life, he will be cheated out of his adolescence. This applied to at least half the population, if not more, who thus lost the mobility and freedom that they should have enjoyed at this time of their lives. From this moment onwards they were part of the economic treadmill, never to leave it again during their working lives.

The result was an abrupt jump from childhood to adulthood, with the phase of adolescence shrinking to a very short period. To see the difference between then and today in all its brutal clarity you have merely to ask yourself the following question: What working man today is fully capable of earning a living at fourteen? The answer is easy. At best the bottom class of the workers, such as the rural proletariat; even the so-called unskilled labourers require a short period of training. But the vast majority of industrial workers need a more thorough induction. The service industries, too, call for higher and higher skills. This produces a situation in which skilled workers do not earn a living wage before the age of twenty-two to twenty-four; the delay is even longer for the professional classes with their varying periods of full-time education.

With the length of education increases the period of economic dependence. It is quite reasonable to identify youth with this state of affairs. Somehow they are always cared for by others, at first by their parents, and later by the state. And when they do earn money, this is mostly only temporary or pays for only part of their needs. Members of certain professions indeed remain dependent up to the age of thirty if not longer. As long as this situation persists youth will last its full psychological span.

We are thus faced with a new paradox. Youth today physically lasts longer than in the past because of changed economic and technological living conditions. It can therefore be said that youth with the complete change in the educational system becomes an increasingly important structural factor in our societies, which is further enhanced by today's growth of youth's self-awareness. Only when a situation exists in which more and more people depend on higher education will the chance of acquiring self-awareness increase; as we have said before, this means specific morals, *weltanschauung*, socio-cultural and political guiding ideas. This extension of the period of youth today leads to the next question: Does it also create a corresponding influence on society as a whole? This is precisely what we want to discuss: we intend to speak not of youth fashions but of their influence on the adult fashions. To be able to appreciate this we must, however, draw a detailed picture of youth.

It is a typical consequence of the extension of youth that it brings about a division into several subgroups; we have at least the early teenagers up to sixteen, and the late ones up to twenty; the twenties too, can be divided into the early and the late ones, the latter forming a transitional group; the more they approach the stage of economic independence the more they will become integrated in the adult group.

On the basis of this differentiation we can now raise the purely statistical question of the numerical size of the group we call youth today. It is indeed astonishingly large, comprising no less than seventeen years compared with the about thirty years of full economic earning power. If we consider the

Second Interlude: Fashion and Anti-fashion 205

enormous fashion potential inherent in these seventeen years we shall without doubt begin to understand that its influence on the rest of society cannot fail to make itself felt and is by no means confined only to the young generation.

Obviously, this is merely the starting point of the detailed investigations. Market research will treat this only as a general framework, comprising a large number of individual more or less well-defined subgroups. Each of the age groups have to be distinguished according to social origin, the financial means at their disposal, level of education, position within their career and in society as a whole. This disposes of the view that it is enough to develop quite generally fashions for youth. A much more sophisticated range is necessary. It is important for us today that youth has a great opportunity of becoming active in the field of fashion; from a structural angle this implies by no means only a linear increase of absolute numbers, but also a change in quality. This qualitative change is an outstanding trend of the present, which, incidentally, is still in the process of further development.

We therefore find a large amount of uncertainty of behaviour. Many of the new forms of fashion are experimental in character. They are, as it were, in search of themselves and of new possibilities, of which they make use every day, sometimes to drop them again very quickly. This has also produced an extreme speeding up of fashion change, so typical of periods of transition and experimenting in fashion. It could almost be said that every week a new fashion detail erupts, only to disappear again by Saturday. Those who have regular contact with young people can no longer close their eyes to the adventurous speed of this ability to change, which is an expression of the elementary fact of hidden highly creative powers straining to be unleashed. They take advantage of all available elements to create something new. Success, of course, is rare, but that is another question. We should, however, try to understand the situation before we analyse it. We must admit that what is unfolding before our eyes is not simply the fashion of youth, but a revolution of youth in fashion, which is something entirely different. This revolution was without doubt latent since the beginning of the century, before it grew to be a focal structural characteristic of our present-day society. It is in fact inviting an almost total change of our entire habits of dressing, habits which have undergone a long and slow development from the Reformation to the nineteenth century, but have probably reached the end of their growth, so that we may anticipate a total change.

We think indeed that modern youth will discard one piece of the old uniform after the other. The general as well as the partial aspects of fashion will change exactly like styles in the arts. Nor is the fact that political demonstration plays a role anything new: the jackets we wear today were once part of a political demonstration; so were the long trousers worn during the French revolution, which replaced the knee breeches worn by the aristocracy. The political background of our dress is that of the protestant, capitalist businessman. With the conversion of the old industrial society into a new form it is possible that the old fashion, too, will disappear.

This obviously does not mean that in the context of a new aim every single fashion change must always have a political significance, although this would without doubt apply during the initial period. Basically, however, it is enough to set a leavening process in motion, so that it presents always new ideas from its own potentialities; for at the very moment when the old standard no longer applies, practically anything will become possible. This by no means precludes the establishment of a new canon of taste. Innumerable experiments are, however, required until it is found. This calls for both active intelligence and luck, because the right ideas do not always occur automatically. The main point is that the decks are clear for new possibilities as they were at the time when what is our fashion today was new.

Second Interlude: Fashion and Anti-fashion 207

The way that modern youth has travelled began with anti-fashion and has reached the preliminaries of a new style of fashion. Immediately after 1945 the beatniks of San Francisco evolved anti-fashion, which we are finding again in the hippies of today. Its sole basis was opposition. Whereas the San Francisco businessman was smartly dressed, the beatnik simply was *not*. Whereas the businessman wanted a white shirt, the hippie wanted a colourful one. As soon as the businessman wore a colourful shirt, the hippie looked for a garish one; he always wanted to be different; in the end, he didn't wear any shirt at all, but a jumper on his bare skin. All these were protests of anti-fashion, and it is easy to find a peg for every anti-fashion to hang on. This has another consequence. The beatnik of 1945 who protested in this way was by no means free from the bourgeois world he fought against, but depended on it in that he converted it into its opposite in every respect. He thus created the counter-uniform to the uniform.

This was only a first, but essential, step. Innumerable fashion ideas were born as a result of these first actions. Soon they no longer were 'against' something, but continued to be consistently creative within the framework of a new idea of fashion.

A good example is the transformation of present-day jewellery. In contrast with the 'precious' jewels of the bourgeois, which were very expensive, new, cheap jewellery is made from thousands of different cheap meterials. Feathers, leaves, seeds, or fruits are threaded on pieces of string. Exotic-looking patterns are created with bits of wire. Everywhere on the busy streets of our cities today we find little stalls where young people make their own 'jewellery' and sell it to passers-by. The monetary value no longer plays a part, only active imagination. Nor is it important any longer to be against something; to become familiar with the artistic potentialities of every material is the main aim. We are firmly convinced that these ideas about jewellery will soon have a very broad popular appeal.

But changes will by no means be confined to accessories. They will become more far-reaching, affecting particularly the men's jacket derived from the fashion of the Puritan age; the first attacks on it were made in the twenties, by, for example, the omission of collars and lapels. But the modification beginning today will certainly be more radical than before, as the experiments with long knitted jackets show, where the man's belt has undergone a completely unexpected metamorphosis or resurrection in innumerable fantastic shapes.

Anti-fashion therefore did not remain an episode, but became the start of a fashion specific of a certain social stratum, in a certain way in opposition to the great masses.

25 Fashion and Mass Consumption

The widest horizon of fashion to become established was mass consumption, which also indicates that the sociology of fashion as a whole forms only part of mass sociology and the social psychology of collective currents. Fashion is not only an important principle of social change but also one of change in attitudes and behaviour of the great masses. This is probably also the most significant and radical difference between the latest style of social spread of fashion and all its predecessors. Up to now only minorities have been involved, in fact the fashion game has essentially been a means of differentiation from the 'common' way of life of the hoi polloi. Today fashion is no longer exclusive, on the contrary it has become a means of adaptation, developing according to a highly specific code, which in spite of all apparent occasional arbitrariness still reveals a very well-defined line.

The essential condition of this change is a comprehensive structural transformation of modern industrial society which could not be more drastic. To appreciate this all we have to do is look at the difference between the industrial society of 1850 and its advanced equivalent of the 1970s. About 1850 Karl Marx and his quite bourgeois contemporary Lorenz von Stein both found a formula for the structure of their contemporary industrial society, which said that society would split into two large, diametrically opposed classes, the bourgeoisie and the proletariat, with the proletariat constituting the overwhelming majority, and the bourgeoisie the ruling minority. This model of society is the last in which a minority is conspicuous as an *élite* with a leadership function. This model, however, asserts above all that the middle classes will in time completely disappear, so that the important intermediate link in the transmission of fashion would also cease to exist. It is obvious that the percolation of culture to the masses must suffer when links of communication, in our case the middle classes, are broken. In terms of fashion this would mean that in a radical realization of this model only the various constituent groups of the top *élite* would enter into fashion rivalry, whereas the rest of society would remain completely indifferent in this respect. At best it could be assumed of this sector that they wear the fashions of the day before yesterday, assuring it of a kind of ghost-like after-life, which, however, could never again create a style of its own; because it is quite unpredictable how in a 'percolated' civilization the fragments of civilizations of different eras will mix.

Many observers during the nineteenth century certainly realized this. Above all John Ruskin about the middle of the century was intensely critical of the aesthetic creative potentialities of society. It was then that the term 'grey masses' of the workers was invented. They were opposed to all civilizing influences; this applied to both men and women. Had the structural model of industrial society of those days not changed, we would be safe to assume that this state of affairs would also have continued unchanged to our days.

But in reality, not only did Karl Marx's and Lorenz von Stein's forecasts not materialize; a new structural model of the advanced industrial societies has developed which, quite unlike its predecessor, is centred not on the lower classes, but on the middle classes in the widest sense. Naturally, upper classes exist even today, but their leadership function, not only in creative fashion, has, as we have seen, largely atrophied. The lower classes, too, have been transformed. Only a small proportion of them consists of workers, that is, the unskilled industrial and farm labourers. These two groups continue to be indifferent to the lure of fashion. The unskilled farm labourers especially still approximate most closely today to the concept of the 'grey masses'. But even combined the two groups are only a minority. The point of gravity of present-day society lies in the centre, and this can easily be proved.

At the beginning of industrial capitalism the most conspicuous feature was the enormous increase in the numbers of unskilled workers. Contemporary observers can hardly be blamed for their assumption that this development would always continue in the same direction but in reality this never happened; the highest proportion the workers ever reached was about 50 per cent of the entire working population. On the other hand, quite considerable adjustments took place within the working class. Of the 50 per cent of the working population 10 per cent were skilled workers compared with 90 per cent who were unskilled, clearly bottom class ones at the time. Today the situation is completely different. Firstly, the working class as a whole tends to remain numerically constant or to decrease slightly. Secondly, the ratio of unskilled to skilled workers has considerably altered. Today the ratio of unskilled to semi-skilled and skilled workers is 20:80. A great many of the skilled workers, technicians and plant engineers, have risen to become members of the middle classes. Moreover the number of workers ceased to increase towards the end of the nineteenth century, while a new social class established itself, whose numerical strength had before been rather insignificant: that of the white-collar workers. From the very beginning these had middle-class pretensions, although occasionally they merely copied the old middle classes. Thus the office worker wore a stiff, white collar like his boss; except that it was made of rubber and was washable. Like his boss, the office worker wore a tiepin with a pearl, except that his pearl was false. All the same, there was this difference between him and the blue-collar worker: he wore a tie, and from the very beginning he skimped and scraped to be able to spend more on his home and above all on clothing at the expense of food. Members of the new white-collar class were typically and strongly preoccupied with clothes and their outward appearance even if at the beginning of the century and during the great economic crisis of 1929 they found the financial strain considerable. The white-collar worker economized in food and thus created a new image of the service occupations in modern society; to the worker eating and drinking were among the most important pleasures of life.

The rapid increase in the numbers of white-collar workers became clearly evident in all European societies at the end of the nineteenth century. Initially the number of office workers increased both absolutely and relatively. But this is of no particular interest. What is important is the relation between employees ('staff') and workers in the modern societies: this has changed drastically since the end of the nineteenth century so that there are now very much fewer workers in proportion to members of staff. This has finally brought about a structural change, so that our modern societies appear fundamentally different from the capitalism of 1850. The upper ranks of the workers take up an increasing share of consumption and of fashion articles; in the field of politics their role has become more important, too. They are joined by the huge army of white-collar workers, from the humble office clerk to the leading executive, who is often a member of the topmost income groups. The characteristic they all share is that they offer their labour on the labour market, in other words, that they are dependent; in this they differ perhaps most significantly from the early form of the old middle classes. This middle class and the remnants of the old middle class, such as artisans, merchants, civil servants, members of the academic professions, still has many other representatives. As a group they form what we now call the mainstay of society; they are also the most important consumers of the mass-produced articles of fashion. They aivdly acquire the means of aesthetic self-expression, transforming this middle stratum of society into something different beyond recognition from that grey mass of the nineteenth century whose potentialities of self-expression were considered so sceptically by their contemporary social critics.

It was the women, particularly the young women, who first took advantage of what the fashion market had to offer. When we look at, for instance, the age of impressionism we find that in France the lower-class female employees began to take an interest in fashion as early as the middle of the nineteenth century. This applies even to working-class girls so that we can claim that the response to fashion has entered the working class through the young girls. The typical picture of a Sunday in Moulin de la Galette shows, cheek-by-jowl with the representatives of the traditional bourgeoisie, the little working girl with her working-class boy friend, who still does not wear a tie, although he may wear a dark suit; the girl, however, takes great pains to compete with the other women, displaying an intensely feminine trait in the fashion-based self-expression of modern man. This feminine trait constituted a tremendous stimulus for the ready-to-wear clothing industry, which owed to it its fantastic rise during the last hundred years. It first produced the light, cheap dress, and developed an enormous range of high-quality dresses which we take for granted today, and which has something to offer for every size of pocket. It is a strange phenomenon that the question of price is of widely varying significance, as the disproportionately high prices of the cosmetics industry and of brand names in underwear from panties to bras show. The aesthetic appeal of these articles seems to ignore economic considerations completely.

In this middle class society a trait of the beginning of the nineteenth century has persisted throughout, particularly in the large cities such as Paris, London, and New York. Whereas the romantic dandy wanted to be conspicuous at all costs, sometimes dyeing his hair purple like Baudelaire and taking a tame lobster on a lead across the Boulevard des Italiens, the rule today is not to be conspicuous, to be reserved although well-dressed. Extremes, as we have said before, are the preserve only of fringe elements; the new middle classes basically regard any eccentricity as bad taste. It must at the same time be said that the specialist technologists who took the lead in the development of the modern mass production of fashion were themselves members of the middle classes and accordingly exerted quite a considerable influence on the style of fashionable self-expression of modern society, in addition to the still increasing trend of perfectionism in today's ready-to-wear fashions. At the same time the distrust by the members of the new middle classes of the quality maintained by the fashion industry disappeared owing to their increasing technical insight and information through the mass media of the daily press, the periodicals, the cinema, and television. In this society the individual is assessed not only according to his income, but above all according to his level of education and outward appearance. This is the basis of the modern style of consumption in the mass society, both in western and socialist societies. Nor are the societies of the Third World excluded, although here it is only the very thin crust of the *elite* whose image has changed.

Even the industry's tendency of spreading a relatively uniform consumer style, a fact closely associated with the technological conditions of mass production, does not by any means imply a drift towards general uniformity – not even on an elevated level, to use a favourite expression of our social critics. Certainly, the radical difference between the old upper class and the lower classes has disappeared. But this does not mean that the minor differences need also disappear. On the contrary, as de Tocqueville observed when in the United States he studied mass civilization for the first time: minor differences can be felt far more strongly when general equality has won the day. It could be said that in the modern mass civilization of the advanced industrial societies it is not the great contrasts, but the delicate differences that are effective; the delicate difference is the most perfect expression of the increasing democratization of society. This applies not only to politics but also to fashion consumption.

26　The Expansion of the Consumer Field

But fashion affects not only the outer shell of clothing, decoration, and adornment, it takes hold of man as a whole; this was our starting point. We can again prove the truth of this assertion by showing that not only do products in some way connected with clothes depend on fashion development, but also countless other items and behaviour patterns and even durable consumer goods provided they are based on industrial mass production. This exposes to the influence of fashion even those items that in the past had been relatively immune to it. The furniture industry is a case in point; architectural design, too, changes more rapidly today, and the rhythm of fashion now affects even the outward appearance of our large cities.

A decisive feature in this situation is the expansion of the consumer field. The various individual forms of consumption have become extraordinarily differentiated. A striking example is foodstuffs. Thorstein Veblen has already shown that the refinement of luxury foods represents an important aspect of their elaboration by fashion. This means that every luxury article of food reaches the market in countless variations trying to satisfy every taste. As a result such qualitative differentiation cannot fail to develop further by producing specialities. Far from leading to uniformity of the products, mass consumption has the exactly opposite effect of a fan-like spread of the field of consumption with an extremely finely graded range of goods to choose from. This applies not only to every single article of luxury food; the quantity of such foods is also increasing considerably. To begin with, luxury food that had formerly been strictly regional has become generally available, such as the oriental marzipan which from Byzantium reached the cities of ancient Russia, via the established trade routes; it spread farther to the Baltic coast, where it became known as a Lübeck speciality, and is now manufactured everywhere. Luxury articles that are also stimulants have especially a tendency of extremely rapid spread, for instance the cigar and the cigarette, which in no time at all became popular throughout the whole world, and hashish and similar drugs in our own days. Other luxury articles, too, spread at the same rate. During his stay at the court of Jenghiz Khan Marco Polo was introduced to a large number of foods new to him, which he took back with him when he returned to Venice; from there they spread to Italy. Spaghetti originated in Mongolia and China; it is now a food known throughout the world that has spread far beyond the borders of Italy. It even changed its function as it did so: to begin with it was a typical poor man's food; today, particularly outside Italy, it has become a symbol of a sophisticated cuisine and is a popular speciality. Today restaurants offering Italian fare have spread as far as the West Coast of the United States. Within the last few years another speciality of the Italian poor, the Neapolitan pizza, has enjoyed a similarly fast rise in popularity. It tastes equally delicious in Naples, Paris, London, New York, San Francisco, Sao Paolo, Buenos Aires, Sydney, and Tokyo.

But the differentiation of consumption basically extends to the entire sophisticated section, 'sophisticated' in this context meaning the aesthetic improvement of those foodstuffs that exclusively serve to meet our biological needs. Sophistication thus began with the refinement and differentiation of consumption, at the moment when man no longer consumed merely to assuage his hunger, but to satisfy at the same time an also felt aesthetic need, which is by no means confined to the individual but has developed in the social intercourse of man. The social development of sophisticated consumption therefore differs from an individual fad: for all the forms of consumption that have social value are also socially standardized.

Strangely enough these forms of consumption are also propagated in directions other than those we have just described. A good example is musical 'consumption', which has indeed undergone quite a number of transformations within the last fifty years, completely changing the attitude of the average person to this form of art. The gramophone was the first thing to bring about this change in that it made it possible to extend the enjoyment of music from the concert hall to the home. Like certain types of food, music, too, is now conserved. The radio has a similar function, although here the listener depends more closely on the programme provided than with the gramophone. On television, too, musical programmes are regularly broadcast. Music is thus performed not only in the concert hall and the opera house, as chamber music in the cultivated home or by the male voice choir; today other means of presenting it exist that were not available in the past. In places where many people congregate regularly, at work, shopping, or in public transport vehicles, they are increasingly exposed to a constant 'irrigation' with background music, which has become a permanent feature of modern life. The industrial production of certain technological appliances has favoured this technically based consumption.

This does not necessarily mean a lowering of standards. On the contrary, if we compare the pathetic and soul-destroying piano performances of the nineteenth-century young ladies or the booze-inspired bawling of male-voice choirs with the performances of the modern record industry and premier broadcasting companies, it will be obvious that in fact a perfectionism has developed that has never existed before.

The Expansion of the Consumer Field

Again, the extremely wide range of information on the programmes of these mass media offered in special publications and an increasing familiarity with these new media allow correspondingly varied kinds of application, so that in this respect, too, we cannot speak of a levelling-down.

The expansion of the consumer field is indeed a significant structural feature of modern society. In other words, this kind of consumption is the result of factors that are inseparable from this society. One of the most important ones is the completely changed form of leisure time. We have already pointed out that leisure, in complete contrast to the past, regularly brings people into the centre of our large cities where they are able to look at the goods offered by the fashion industry. In addition, entirely new needs are created in that man today not only consumes to recover the energy expended during work; the consumption of certain products becomes an activity in its own right quite independently of its original purpose.

We can say without exaggeration that tourism with all its ramifications constitutes such a profound modification of the old ways of life. We are not thinking of the old individual tourism, which, for instance, sent the sons of great aristocratic families on the 'grand tour'; what interests us is mass tourism. The equivalent of the mass production of modern production industry is the orientation of the service industries towards the mass of holidaymakers; an additional stimulus is the French legislation which introduced paid holidays in the twenties, a necessary further development of the limit on working hours in modern industry. When Karl Marx called the eight-hour day the 'victory of a principle' he had little idea of its consequences during the latter part of the twentieth century.

This aspect of leisure consumption has without doubt many playful features. It corresponds to the freedom provided by leisure, but also exerts a tremendous pressure on the sphere of production. All goods that play a part in leisure pursuits are also most widely open to the influence of fashion. A vast new range of behaviour patterns, goods, and kinds of enjoyment, of a thoroughly aesthetic nature as well as obeying the laws of fashion in the changeability of its forms, thus opens up beyond the world of industry and work.

27 The New Line

Modern social critics regularly take up a very negative stance here, and depict the new forms of consumption, without doubt considerably expanded in modern times, simply as an expression of insatiable greed. Even theoreticians sometimes display an attitude that is anything but unbiased. They regularly apply, for instance, the theoretical model of the economy – which functions very well for the whole of the economy and states that in the market place the principles of the 'unlimited' needs of man are opposed to limited (scarce) resources – to the attitude of the individual consumer. They thereby commit several errors, above all forgetting that the economy today is no longer based on scarcity, but on the control of surplus. It is also completely wrong to think that the needs of the final consumer are unlimited, for the behaviour of the average man is never totally free-ranging, but formed by habit, customs, tradition and lastly by fashion. The situation in real consumption is by no means one in which an isolated economic unit is confronted with almost limitless supply, so that it could simply be persuaded to buy, buy, buy; to consume, in fact, still means to choose, to select from a wide range of possibilities existing today even among the simplest essentials of life. In the real market, in which we make our daily decisions, we do not primarily react like the theoretician's abstract economic units, but mainly as socio-cultural beings; this means, however, that our needs in this field are by no means fundamentally unlimited;

on the contrary, they are always socially and culturally determined and at the same time clearly restricted by the rules of respectability. Fashion-oriented behaviour thus leads not only to selectivity, but also to self-limitation, because any mode of life imposes restrictions. This alone eliminates, at least in part, a source of very weighty prejudices. We are therefore unable to accept the notion of a limitless 'increase of the desire to own', although we must admit the possibility that consumption styles change, even if this change is slow, and that above all they may expand considerably. But since all consumption is habit-forming and also subject to cultural standardization we can assume from the very outset that after all, and possibly even sudden, changes life will return to relatively settled styles.

This raises once again the question in what conditions are such styles able to change. Here, too, the social critics advance an argument which most of us accept although on more detailed examination it proves to be highly questionable. For most of these critics simply decide that the dominant cause of a change in the consumer style is engineered by the 'hidden persuaders', the adman. Now we do not at all wish to discount the idea that advertising plays an important part in the advanced industrial societies; it is the nature of this role which is in doubt.

All advertising first passes through the filter of old-established habits and the generally acknowledged standards of consumption, whose great importance to the arrangement of day-to-day life we have already recognized. Advertising itself is therefore subject to fashion impulses. Far from inducing fashion changes itself, the change in the style of advertising is usually the first symptom of a fashion change that has already taken place. What in the abstract is regarded as a cause is really the effect.

In addition, the impulses generated by advertising encounter other collectively held views, such as the prejudices of the social classes (consumer styles differ in the upper, middle, and lower classes), or the consumer styles of various cultural regions (northern, southern, eastern Europe), as well as the differences between general styles of life, such as urban and rural civilization, life on the coast and inland, on the plains and in mountain country. In all these cases conceptions, aversions, predilections are not private or individual, but collectively formed traditions, some of which have been established for a considerable time.

Apart from these comprehensive group relations, which form fixed habits, there are numerous smaller groups which are equally important for the nature of consumption. These are above all the family group, the group of adults at work, and among adolescents of both sexes above all people of the same age.

Here the questions of consumption, modesty, etiquette, tact and taste are discussed in great detail. The result is again a definite deflection and transformation of the impulses produced by advertising owing to the fact that they hardly ever reach isolated individuals, but almost always groups with socially formed conceptions and habits which carefully sift these external stimuli. Here the discussion of the various advantages and disadvantages of the products offered plays an important part. Family discussion thus becomes an important means of ascertaining the market situation; it is therefore completely wrong to claim that the average consumer is a defenceless victim of the powers of the economy. On the contrary: every product on the market has to surmount these cultural and social barriers imposed on consumption before it is accepted. Among those responsible there is a growing appreciation of this situation; increasing use is made of market and opinion surveys to gain an insight into the interplay of the forces motivating the consumer on which the success of a product depends in the last resort. The notion of a completely irresistible 'manipulation' of the consumer must therefore be utterly rejected.

Under the impact of these facts advertising has changed

considerably during the last twenty-five years. Today it not so much sings the praises of its object (the best, biggest, finest, cheapest, etc.) but begins with straightforward, simple information about the new consumer product, fitting it into everyday life. In addition, advertising increasingly tends to change its role from that of mere information to becoming part of the consumer product itself; for instance in the form of an attractive wrapper or of the adoption of industrial design principles to give the product a pleasing look in accordance with the new style – this last point applies particularly to the more durable consumer goods from furniture to household appliances, from fountain pens to motorcars. Here the advertising effect originates in the product itself, which through its novel design becomes part of modern civilization. The streamlined shape is in this respect more than an element of form: it is the self-expression of certain products as socially accepted elements of consumption in the new style of the advanced industrial society with its new principles of product design.

The final product of this new style of living is the 'expectation' with which the various groups of society approach life itself and what the market has to offer. This expectation determines the choice from the immense range of goods available and also the quantitative relation between products. This applies particularly to the ratio between expenditure in the family budget on food and on the equipment and size of the home, on clothing, education, and cultural and leisure requirements. Nothing contradicts the uncritical assumption of the unlimited multiplication of our demands so much as the striking regularities of the limitation of expenditure on food compared with other items.

Man's hunger is indeed quickly appeased. This has an interesting result: where there is a general rise in real income, as in all democratic industrial societies, the part of the family budget spent on food progressively shrinks. Consequently the resources available for improvements to the home or for other consumer goods immediately increase. Thus a gradual shift of emphasis occurs on the market, which is typical of the advanced industrial societies in that a whole new range of possibilities of consumption is opened up. It is precisely in this situation that more and more goods that have advanced from positions on the fringe of everyday life to principal positions on the market accepted by the great masses are being drawn into the orbit of fashion design.

Apart from introducing beauty into lives that for the majority of us have become difficult and relentless, and from its playfulness, which provides us with a welcome freedom in a world of compulsion and necessity, fashion has today become one of the most important media for the self-expression of the great masses. This is certainly its foremost achievement. With the typical and modest means at its disposal fashion is indeed capable of imprinting a characteristic stamp on the seemingly chaotic masses of present-day society and thereby of providing them with a starting point for their formative progress.

Select Bibliography

It is not our intention to provide an exhaustive reference of literature on fashion. Since the number of authors that have written on this subject is legion such a list of references would go far beyond what can reasonably be expected within the framework of this book. We must moreover point out that such a comprehensive list would also have to contain the many asides which are found among the works of poets, novelists, writers and social critics of all kinds and which are sometimes more revealing than fat volumes. After all, the fascination of the phenomenon of fashion is so great that its effects are encountered everywhere and that we cannot remain indifferent to it. We are therefore mentioning, under the heading of each chapter, only those works which have either been quoted directly, or which have provided the author with important material.

For and Against Fashion
William Gr. Sumner, *Folkways. A Study of the Sociological Importance of Usages, Manners, Customs, Mores, and Morals*, 2nd edn., Boston, 1913; Sigmund Freud, *Vorlesungen zur Einfuehrung in die Psychoanalyse* (Introductory lectures in psychoanalysis), in: *Gesammelte Schriften*, Band VII (Collected writings, Vol. VII), Leipzig-Vienna-Zurich, 1924; id., *Totem and Tabu*, in: Ges. Schriften, Band X (Collected writings, Vol. X), Leipzig-Vienna-Zurich, 1924; J. C. lugel, *The Psychology of Clothes*, 3rd edn., London, 1950; Edmund Bergler, *Fashion and the Unconscious*, New York, 1923; Ingrid Brenninkmeyer, *The Sociology of Fashion*, Opladen, 1963.

Fashion-oriented Behaviour – Content and Form
On fashion as a short-term change, mainly S. R. Steinmetz, *Die Mode* (Fashion), in: *Gesammelte kleinere Schriften zur Ethnologie und Soziologie*, Band III (Collected short essays on ethnology and sociology, Vol. III), Groningen, 1935; cf. the article 'Mode' by the same author in

Handwoerterbuch der Soziologie (Dictionary of sociology), edited by A. Vierkandt, Stuttgart, 1931.

Recent histories of fashion
J. Laver, *Style in Costume*, London, 1949; H. H. Hansen, *Histoire du Costume* (History of dress), Paris, 1956.

The All-embracing Reality of Fashion
Stendhal wrote already about the process of crystallization in his *Essai sur l'amour* (Essay on love), 1822. A. L. Kroeber, *Order in Changes in Fashion*, and, *Three Centuries of Women's Dress Fashions: A Quantitative Analysis*, both in: *The Nature of Culture*, Chicago, 1952.

Change and Stability
cf. above all the already mentioned works by S. R. Steinmetz; Richard Alewyn, *Formen des Barock* (Forms of the baroque), in: *Corona* X, 6. Roland Barthes, *Système de la mode* (System of fashion), Paris 1967.

Roots and Branches
On the 'imposition' of fashion on certain general human (anthropological) basic conditions cf. Nicolai Hartmann, *Das Problem des geistigen Seins* (The problem of intellectual existence), Berlin, 1932.

Fashion-oriented Behaviour in Animals and Children
On the games of apes and monkeys, cf. Wolfgang Koehler, Karl Groos and others. On the behaviour of children, mainly the various works by Jean Piaget. On the smile, Georges Dumas, *Le Sourire. Psychologie et physiologie* (The smile. Its psychology and physiology), Paris, 1906; Helmuth Plessner, *Lachen und Weinen* (Laughing and Crying), Munich, 1950. Konrad Lorenz, *Ueber tierisches und menschliches Verhalten*, 2 Baende (Animal and human behaviour, 2 vols), Munich, 1965; W. H. Thorpe, 'The Concept of Ritualisation' in: W. H. Thorpe and O. L. Zangwill, *Current Problems in Animal Behaviour*, Cambridge, 1961; I. Eibl-Eibesfeld, *Grundrisse der vergleichenden Verhaltensforschung* (Outlines of comparative ethology), Munich, 1967.

Novelty, Curiosity, and the New Look
On the problem of curiosity cf. mainly Hans von Blarer, *Die Neugier* (Curiosity), Basle, 1951.

To See and to be Seen
Sigmund Freud, *Zur Einfuehrung des Narzissmus* (The introduction of narcissism), in: Gesammelte Schriften, Band VI (Collected writings, Vol. VI), Leipzig-Vienna-Zurich, 1925.

Decoration and Distinction
Richard Thurnwald, *Werden, Wandel und Gestaltung von Staat und Kultur* (Growth, change, and formation of the state and culture), Berlin and Leipzig, 1935; Herbert Spencer, *Die Prinzipien der Soziologie* (Principles of sociology, 4 vols), Stuttgart, undated, especially Vol. III, Pt. 4: 'Die Herrschaft des Ceremoniells' (The rule of ceremonial); on the term 'ornamental money' see Wilhelm Gerloff, *Die Entstehung des Geldes und die Anfaenge des Geldwesens* (The origin of money and the beginnings of the monetary system), Frankfurt, 1940, 3rd edn., 1947; John Adair, *The Navajo and Pueblo Silversmiths*, University of Oklahoma Press, 1965.

Recognition
This aspect of fashion was described above all by Fausto Squillage, *La moda* (fashion), Rome, 1912.
On children's clothing: Recently Philippe Aries, *L'enfant et la vie familiale* (The child and family life), Paris 1960.

Rivalry and Competition
On potlatch cf., Marcel Mauss, 'Essai sur le don' (Essay on presents), reprinted in the collective volume *Sociologie et anthropologie*, Paris, 1950; George Davy, *La foi jurée* (The sworn faith), Paris, 1922; id., *Des clans aux empires* (From clans to empires), Paris, 1923; Jean Huizinga, *Homo Ludens*, Basle, 1939; Helen Codere, *Fighting with Property*, New York, 1950; Ruth Benedict, *Patterns of Culture*, first published 1934, Mentor Books, 1946; Thorstein Veblen, *The Theory of the Leisure Class*, first published 1899.

Conspicuousness and Approval
Edmond Goblot, *La barrière et le niveau* (The barrier and the standard), Paris, 1925.

Imitation
Gabriel Tarde, *Les lois de l'imitation* (The laws of imitation), Paris, 1890; Georg Simmel, *Philosophie der Mode* (The philosophy of fashion), Berlin, 1905.

Performers and Spectators
Alfred Vierkandt, *Gesellschaftslehre* (Sociology), 2nd edn., Stuttgart, 1928.

Ceremonial Behaviour and Etiquette
cf. the already-mentioned works by W. Gr. Sumner, N. Spencer, etc.

The Process of Civilization and Modesty
J. Haesaert, *Etiologie de la rèpression des outrages publics aux bonnes moeurs* (Etiology of the suppression of public offences against morality) Paris, 1931; Norbert Elias, *Ueber den Prozess der Zivilisation* (The process of civilization, 2 vols), Basle, 1939, new edn. Berne-Munich, 1969.

The First Spread of Fashion-Oriented Behaviour
cf. the various histories of fashion by Max von Boehn and other authors.

Fashion in the Bourgeois Moneyed Circles
Nineteenth century cf. especially Dolf Sternberger, *Panorama*, 2nd edn., Frankfurt, 1956.

Male Puritanism Versus Female Fashion
On the problem of puritanism in the modern economic society generally cf. the works by Max Weber and his successors. René Koenig, 'Mode und Erotik' (Fashion and eroticism), in: R. Koenig, *Soziologische Orientierungen* (Sociological orientations), Cologne, 1965.

On the importance of Jacques Offenbach
Siegfried Kracauer, *J. Offenbach und das Paris seiner Zeit* (J. Offenbach and the Paris of his time), Amsterdam, 1937; Alphons Silbermann, *Das imaginaere Tagebuch des Herrn Jacques Offenbach* (The imaginary diary of M. Jacques Offenbach), Berlin-Wiesbaden, 1960.

Fashion Captures the Masses
cf. generally the various structural analyses of modern society, e.g. René Koenig, *Soziologie heute* (Sociology today), Zurich, 1949. id., *Soziologie der Grosstadt* (Sociology of the large city), in: R. Koenig, editor of *Handbuch der empirischen Sozialforschung*, Bd. 2, (Handbook of empirical social research, Vol. 2), Stuttgart, 1969. On cosmetics: Hans Freytag, *Die soziale Bedeutung der Kosmetik* (The social significance of cosmetics), in: *Parfümerie und Kosmetik* (Perfumery and cosmetics, Vol. 52), 1971. cf. also W. E. J. Schneidrzik, *Kosmetische Chirurgie* (Cosmetic surgery), Duesseldorf, 1970. Also R. Koenig, *Kosmetik als sozio-kulturelles Problem* (Cosmetics as a socio-cultural problem), in *Kosmetologie* (Cosmetology, I), 1971.

The Spread of Fashion in Today's Society
Paul Nystroem, *Economics of Fashion*, New York, 1928.

Fashion and Mass Consumption
Ernest Zahn, *Soziologie der Prosperitaet* (The sociology of prosperity);

Wirtschaft und Gesellschaft in Zeichen des Wohlstandes (Economy and society in the age of affluence), Munich dtv 1964 (first published Cologne, 1960). René Koenig, *Soziologische Orientierungen* (Sociological orientations), Cologne, 1965. Erwin K. Scheuch, *Soziologie der Freizeit* (The sociology of leisure), in: R. Koenig, *Handbuch*... (*Handbook*..., Vol. 2).

Subject Index

absenteeism 111
absolutism 141
age 176
agonistics 102
ambivalent behaviour 33
anti-fashion 65, 198

barrier 112, 114, 119, 148, 153
beard fashions 49
Beatles 200
Beatle haircut 47
beatniks 172, 199
blousons noirs 172
bourgeoisie, urban 141

ceremonial behaviour 128
change and adaptation 54
childrens' dress 97
class system, bourgeois 147
city 179
civilization, process of 133
cliques 126
clothing 91
  working 173
commensuality 108
competition 101, 106, 122
conspicuousness 111, 112
conspicuous consumption 106
consumption of music 218
cosmetics and cosmetics industry 74, 173

counter effect 56
courtesy 131
courts 58, 131, 136, 143
craze 42, 46
createur 152
crystallization 41, 55
curiosity 76
custom 61

dandy 151, 162
dead stock 124
decoration 84
delicate differences and democratization 215
democratization 38, 215
displacement 35, 44, 54, 66, 82, 93
distinction 113, 149
dress 36, 96, 98
  and social rank 98
  occupational 98
  regulations 99
dummy experiments 73
dynamism, social 38

eroticism 36, 81, 93, 133, 173
etiquette 113, 128, 137, 141, 148, 149, 157, 167, 223
examples 151
exhibitionism 57, 133

fad 42, 47
fancy fashions 144
fashion
  abortive 52, 152, 180
  childrens' 97
  germinal forms 71
    with children 69
  class 98
  definition 40, 54, 61, 128
  effect on human body 48, 95
  faulty solutions 51
  fluctuations 43
  form of fashion-oriented behaviour 37
  latent effect 181
  pendulum swing 41
  pioneers 152, 172
  rage 47
  roots 66
  sales 124, 183
  secular rhythm 42
  self-destruction 123
  as social regulator 45
  as social change 45
  show 59, 184
  spread 165, 176
  standstill 88
    and style 40, 43
  with animals 69
  versatility 53
feminine style 162
festivities 59, 102
feudalism 58, 101, 109, 136, 139, 141, 154
folk costume 67, 90, 94, 120, 128
  books on 140
fop 151
French revolution 43, 146, 152, 158, 206
fringe elements 62, 151

gadget 46
gammler 172
guaglioni 172

Halbstarke 172
happening 199
hippies 48, 172, 207
history of dress 40
hobby 125, 126
hot pants 44

imitation 116
improvement methods 182
inquisitive behaviour in animals 77
insecurity (fringe) 62, 125,
  interieur style 164

jewellery 202
jumper 190, 207

knitwear 186

lady 50
leisure wear 191
light, role of in modern life style 167
loafers 199

machismo 144
make-up 74, 173
male and female dress (difference between) 97
male dress 48, 97, 154, 159
man-made fibres 192
manners 135
mass consumption 209
  media 59, 168
masses 165
maxi-look 44
middle classes 210
mini-skirt 44, 56

Subject Index

mobility, social 166
modesty 91, 133
moneyed circles, bourgeois 146
monopoly of opinion 42

neckline, plunging 43, 135, 194
New Look 56, 76, 159
nudism (birthday suit) 50

Olympic Games 189
organic neurosis 175
ornamental money 87

Paris, fashion leadership of 179
performers and spectators (exchange of roles between) 122
pheniatry 174
poses 47
Potlatch ceremony 102, 105, 108
power and fashion 142
presents 104
prestige economy 105
provos 172
publicity 42
puritanism 154

quality, new concept of 182

ready-to-wear clothing 165, 184
recognition 95
reference group 63
refinement 107
relative underprivilege 63
revulsion 133
ritualization 74, 114

scene 57
scents 74
short term 46
signal period 56, 61, 167
silk industry 185
smile 72
snob 62, 124
stage 57
standard 119, 148
staple consumer goods 42
sumptuary laws 111, 139
synthetic fibres 192

tact 113, 131, 223
taste 113, 153
teddy boys 63
teenagers 204
time off 191
topless dress 193
to see and to be seen 75
trigger 72
trophies 86, 91
trouser suit 44
twenties 204

uncertainty 152
uniformity 64, 97, 113, 165

waist string 92
wealth 86, 87, 107, 136, 149, 177
weaving 186
white-collar workers 211
white elephants 124
woman as consumer 159, 176

youth 190, 198, 200, 202, 203

Name Index

Abraham a Santa Clara 32
Achilles 97
Adair, John 31
Aelian 31
Aldegrever, Heinrich 140
Alewyn, Richard 58, 155
Alexander the Great 31
Amman, Jost 140
Ascham, Roger 31

Balbo, Italo 49
Balzac, Honoré de 149
Bardot, Brigitte 70
Barthes, Roland 39
Baudelaire, Charles 32, 214
Benedict, Ruth 106
Bleuler, Eugen 33
Boehn, Max von 136
Boissard, J. J. 140
Boussac, Marcel 198
Brummell, Beau 162
Bruyn, Abraham 140

Carracci, Agostino 61
Castiglione, Baldassarre 141
Charlemagne 139
Charles V 142, 155
Charles VII 194
Charles the Bold 58
Codere, Helen 105

Dior, Christian 198
Disraeli, Benjamin 163
Duerer, Albrecht 135
Dumas-Fils, Alexandre 163

Edward VII (Prince of Wales) 59, 121, 170
Elias, Norbert 135, 136
Elizabeth I 31
Erasmus of Rotterdam 137
Eugénie, Empress of France 59

Flugel, J. C. 36
Francis Joseph, Emperor of Austria 49
Freud, Sigmund 33, 35, 81, 83
Freytag, Hans 174

Garbo, Greta 170
Garibaldi, Giuseppe 49
George IV 162
Goblot, Edmond 112, 114, 148, 153
Goethe, Johann Wolfgang v. 31
Goncourt, Edmond and Jule de 32, 81
Goya, Francisco 89
Graf, Urs 144
Greco, Juliette 50, 190, 198

Haesaert, J. P. 133
Hals, Frans 156
Hercules 49
Horace 31, 57
Huizinga, Jan 102

Isaiah 29, 32

Jacquard, Joseph-Marie 186
Jaeger, Gustav 187
Jenghis Khan 217

Kroeber, Alfred L. 42–4, 46

Lamb, Isaac W. 188
Lee, William 187
Lenglen, Suzanne 189
Lessing, Gotthold Ephraim 32
Lorenz, Konrad 70, 73
Louis XIV 109, 143, 179
Lycomedes 97

Mallarmé, Stéphane 32
Mandeville, Bernard de 30
Marx, Karl 209, 219
Mauss, Marcel 104
de' Medici Catherine 157
    Cosimo 141
    Lorenzo (Il Magnifico) 141
Meng, Heinrich 175
Michelangelo 156
Moscherosch, Joh. Michael 32

Napoleon III 163
Nystroem, Paul 180, 181

Offenbach, Jacques 163

Peleus 97
Petrarch (Petrarca, Francesco) 51
Philip the Good 58

Plato 120
Polo, Marco 217
Poussin, Nicolas 61

Quant, Mary 44

Récamier, Madame de 194
Reinhardt, Max 59
Rembrandt 156
Ruskin, John 210

Sartre, Jean-Paul 198
Savonarola, Girolamo 31, 58
Schiller, Friedrich v. 31
Schneidrzik, W. E. J. 175
Schnitzler, Arthur 82
Schopenhauer, Arthur 161
Schwarz, Matthaeus and Veit
    Konrad 140
Scribe, Eugéne 163
Shakespeare, William 9, 47, 156, 200
Simmel, Georg 116, 117
Socrates 31
Sorel, Agnes 194
Spencer, Herbert 86, 99, 100, 116, 117
Stein, Lorenz von 209
Steinmetz, S. R. 54, 100, 128, 137
Strauss, Levi 171
Sumner, William Graham 29

Talleyrand, Prince 194
Tarde, Gabriel 116
Titian 155
Tocqueville, Alexis de 214

Ulysses 97

Veblen, Thorstein 106, 108, 143, 158, 216

Vico, Enea 140
Victoria, Queen 126, 163
Vierkandt, Alfred 122
Vischer, Friedrich Theodor 32, 136

Wagner, Richard 59

Wilde, Oscar 32
Wilhelm II, German Emperor 49

Xanthippe 31

Zephaniah 29